KENNETH LEE PIKE BIBLIOGRAPHY

ARCADIA BIBLIOGRAPHICA

VIRORUM ERUDITORUM

Editor: Gyula Décsy

Fasciculus 10

Kenneth Lee Pike

Bibliography

Compiled

by

RUTH M. BREND

EUROLINGUA

Eurasian Linguistic Association

Bloomington, Indiana 47402-0101

1987

Kenneth Lee Pike

Bibliography

Compiled

by

RUTH M. BREND

EUROLINGUA
Eurasian Linguistic Association
Bloomington, Indiana 47402-0101

1987

Library of Congress Catalog Card Number: 87-80515

Manufactured in the United States of America

ISSN 0195-7163   ISBN 0-931922-28-3

Kenneth L. Pike

Table of Contents

1. BOOKS

1.1 Linguistics

1.1.1 *A Reconstruction of Phonetic Theory.* University of Michigan. Ph.D. Dissertation. 1941, 229 pp.

1.1.2 *Pronunciation.* Vol. 1 of *An Intensive Course in English for Latin American Students.* Ann Arbor: English Language Institute of the University of Michigan, 1942. 85 pp.

1.1.3 *Phonetics: a Critical Analysis of Phonetic Theory and a Technic for the Practical Description of Sounds.* University of Michigan Publications in Language and Literature 21. Ann Arbor: University of Michigan Press, 1943, ix + 182 pp. Revised version of No. 1.1.1.

1.1.4 *The Intonation of American English.* University of Michigan Publications in Linguistics 1. Ann Arbor: University of Michigan Press, 1945, xi + 200 pp.

1.1.5 *Phonemics: A Technique for Reducing Languages to Writing.* University of Michigan Publications in Linguistics 3. Ann Arbor: University of Michigan Press, 1947, xvi + 254 pp. Also 1961, 1963.

1.1.6 *Tone Languages: A Technique for Determining the Number and Type of Pitch Contrasts in a Language, with Studies in Tonemic Substitution and Fusion.* University of Michigan Publications in Linguistics 4. Ann Arbor: University of Michigan Press, 1948, xii + 187 pp. Also 1961, 1964.

1.1.7 *Axioms and Procedures for Reconstruction in Comparative Linguistics: An Experimental Syllabus.* Santa Ana [now Huntington Beach], Calif.: Summer Institute of Linguistics, 1951, 32 pp.; Revised, 1957, 25 pp.

1.1.8 *Language in Relation to a Unified Theory of the Structure of Human Behavior,* Part I, 1955, 170 pp.; Part II, 1955, 85 pp.; Part II, 1960, 146 pp. Glendale [now Huntington Beach], Calif.: Summer Institute of Linguistics. (2nd ed. rev. The Hague: Mouton, 1967, 762 pp., Janua Linguarum Series maior 24).

1.1.9 [and EUNICE U. PIKE]: *Live Issues in Descriptive Lingusitic Analysis.* Glendale, Calif.: Summer Institute of Linguistics, 1955, iv + 23 pp.

1.1.10   *Tagmemic and Matrix Linguistics Applied to Selected African Languages.* (Final Report, Contract OE 5-14-065) Washington, D.C.: U.S. Office of Education, 1966, 289 pp. Reprinted: 1970 in Summer Institute of Linguistics Publications in Linguistics and Related Fields 23 – Appendix omitted, 122 pp.

1.1.11   [and YOUNG, RICHARD E.; and BECKER, ALTON L.]: *Rhetoric: Discovery and Change.* New York: Harcourt, Brace and World, 1970, xxi + 383 pp.

1.1.12   [and HALE, AUSTIN (eds.)]: *Tone Systems of Tibeto-Burman Languages of Nepal.* Part I: Studies on Tone and Phonological Segments; Part II: Lexical Lists and Comparative Studies; Part III: Texts I; Part IV: Texts II. Occasional Papers of the Wolfenden Society on Tibeto-Burman Linguistics, Vol. III. Urbana: University of Illinois, 1970. [Currently available in microfiche from SIL]

1.1.13   *On Describing Language.* Lisse: De Ridder Press, 1975, 35 pp.

1.1.14   *Kenneth L. Pike: Selected Writings.* To commemorate the 60th birthday of Kenneth Lee Pike. Ed. RUTH M. BREND. The Hague: Mouton, 1972, 336 pp.

1.1.15   [and SUHARNO, IGNATIUS (eds.)]: *From Baudi to Indonesian.* Jayapura, Irian Jaya, Indonesia: Cenderawasih University and the Summer Institute of Linguistics, 1976, 209 pp.

1.1.16   [and BREND, RUTH M. (eds.)]: *Tagmemics: Aspects of the Field.* Vol. 1: *Tagmemics: Theoretical Discussion,* 147 pp.; Vol. 2: *Aspects of the Field,* 133 pp. The Hague: Mouton, 1976. Trends in Linguistics. Studies and Monographs 1-2.

1.1.17   [and BREND RUTH M. (eds.)]: *The Summer Institute of Linguistics: Its Works and Contributions.* The Hague: Mouton, 1977, viii + 200 pp.

1.1.18   [and PIKE, EVELYN G.]: *Grammatical Analysis.* Summer Institute of Linguistics Publications in Linguistics 53. Dallas, Texas: Summer Institute of Linguistics and University of Texas at Arlington, 1977, xxix + 505 pp. (2nd ed., 1982, 463 pp.).

1.1.19   [and PIKE EVELYN G.]: *Instructor's Guide for Use with Grammatical Analysis.* Huntington Beach, Calif.: Summer Institute of Linguistics, 1977.

1.1.20   *A Mixtec Lime Oven.* Summer Institute of Linguistics Museum of Anthropology No. 10. Dallas, Texas: Summer Institute of Linguistics, 1980, 9 pp.

1.1.21 *Tagmemics, Discourse, and Verbal Art.* Michigan Studies in the Humanities, ed. RICHARD BAILEY, Ann Arbor: University of Michigan, 1981, xvi + 67 pp. Michigan Studies in the Humanities.

1.1.22 [and PIKE EVELYN G.]: *Grammatical Analysis,* 2nd. ed. Summer Institute of Linguistics Publications in Linguistics 53. Dallas, Texas: Summer Institute of Linguistics and University of Texas at Arlington, 1982, xxvi + 463 pp.

1.1.23 *Linguistic Concepts: An Introduction to Tagmemics.* Lincoln: University of Nebraska Press, 1982, xvi + 146 pp.

1.1.24 [and PIKE EVELYN G.]: *Text and Tagmeme.* Norwood, New Jersey: Ablex, 1983, 129 pp. Open Linguistics Series.

1.2 Religious

1.2.1 [and STARK, DONALD; PIKE, EVELYN; and MERECIAS, ANGEL]: *Cuendú Nda⌐[True Tales]* (in Mixteco). México, D.F.: Instituto Lingüístico de Verano, 1946.

1.2.2 [and MERECIAS, ANGEL]: *La Epístola del Apóstol San Pablo a los Filipenses.* (diglot, Mixteco-Spanish). México, D.F.: Sociedad Bíblica Americana, 1947.

1.2.3 [and STARK, DONALD; and MERECIAS, ANGEL]: *El Santo Evangelio según San Marcos.* (diglot, Mixteco-Spanish). México, D.F.: Sociedad Bíblica Americana, 1947.

1.2.4 [and STARK, DONALD]: *Las Epístolas de San Juan Apóstol* (diglot, Mixteco-Spanish). México, D.F., 1950.

1.2.5 [and STARK, DONALD; and MERECIAS, ANGEL]: *El Nuevo Testamento do Nuestro Señor Jesucristo.* (diglot, Mixteco-Spanish). Cuernavaca, México: Tipografía Indígenia, 1951.

1.2.6 [and STARK, DONALD]: *El Santo Evangelio según San Juan.* (diglot, Mixteco-Spanish). Cuernavaca, México: Tipografía Indígenia, 1957.

1.2.7 [and STARK, DONALD]: *Los Hechos de los Apóstoles.* (diglot, Mixteco-Spanish). Cuernavaca, México: Tipografía Indígenia, 1960.

1.2.8 *With Heart and Mind: A Personal Synthesis of Scholarship and Devotion.* Grand Rapids, Mich.: Wm. B. Eerdmans Publishing Co., 1962, xii + 140 pp.

1.2.9 *Stir-Change-Create: Poems and Essays in Contemporary Mood for Concerned Students.* Grand Rapids, Mich.: W. B. Eerdmans Publishing Co., 1967, 164 pp.

1.2.10 *Mark My Words.* Grand Rapids, Mich.: Wm. B. Eerdmans Publishing Co., 1971, 123 pp.

1.2.11 [and PIKE, STEPHEN B.]: *Songs of Fun and Faith.* (By Fish and Chip, words by Kenneth L. Pike, music by Stephen B. Pike.) Edward Sapir Monograph Series in Language, Culture, and Cognition 1. Supplement to *Forum Linguisticum* 1:3. Lake Bluff, Ill.: Jupiter Press, 1977, viii + 48 pp.

2. ARTICLES AND PAMPHLETS

2.1 Linguistics

2.1.1 "Likenesses, Differences and Variations of Phonemes in Mexican Indian Languages and How To Find Them," *Investigaciones Lingüísticas* 4:1-2(1937).134-139.

2.1.2 "Una Leyenda Mixteca." *Investigaciones Lingüísticas* 4:3-4(1937). 262-270.

2.1.3 "Practical Suggestions Toward a Common Orthography for Indian Languages of Mexico." *Investigaciones Lingüísticas* 5:1-2(1938).86-97.

2.1.4 *Phonemic Work Sheet.* Santa Ana [now Huntington Beach], Calif.: Summer Institute of Linguistics, 1938. Reprinted 1977, *Grammatical Analysis,* pp. 469-474, Dallas Summer Institute of Linguistics and University of Texas at Arlington, 1938.

2.1.5 "Taxemes and Immediate Constituents." *Language* 19(1943).65-82.

2.1.6 "Analysis of a Mixteco Text." *International Journal of American Linguistics* 10(1944).113-138. Reprinted 1972, *Kenneth L. Pike: Selected Writings,* pp. 11-31.

2.1.7 "Mock Spanish of a Mixteco Indian." *International Journal of American Linguistics* 11(1945).219-224.

2.1.8 [and TRAVER, AILEEN; and FRENCH, VIRGINIA]: "Step-by-Step Procedure for Marking Limited Intonation with its Related Features of Pause, Stress, and Rhythm." *Teaching and Learning English as a Foreign Language* by CHARLES C. FRIES. Ann Arbor: English Language Institute, University of Michigan, 1945, pp. 62-74.

2.1.9 "Tone Puns in Mixteco." *International Journal of American Linguistics* 11(1945).129-139.

2.1.10 "The Flea: Melody Types and Perturbations in a Mixtec Song." *Tlalocan* 2(1946).128-133.

2.1.11 "Another Mixteco Tone Pun." *International Journal of American Linguistics* 12(1946).22-24. Reprinted: 1975. *Studies in Tone and Intonation*, ed. RUTH M. BREND. Basel: S. Karger, pp. 57-61.

2.1.12 "Phonemic Pitch in Maya." *International Journal of American Linguistics* 12(1946).82-88.

2.1.13 [and MERECIAS, ANGEL; and other Mixtecs]: *Cuendu Nanga* [Funny Stories]. México, D.F.: Lingüístico de Verano.

2.1.14 "A Text Involving Inadequate Spanish of Mixteco Indians." *International Journal of American Linguistics* 13(1947).251-257.

2.1.15 "On the Phonemic Status of English Diphthongs." *Language* 23(1947).151-159. Reprinted: 1972, *Phonological Theory: Evolution and Current Practice*. ed. VALERIE BECKER MAKKAI. N.Y.: Holt, Rinehart and Winston, Inc., pp. 145-151.

2.1.16 "Grammatical Prerequisites to Phonemic Analysis." *Word* 3(1947). 155-172. Reprinted: 1972. *Kenneth L. Pike: Selected Writings*. The Hague: Mouton, pp. 32-50. Reprinted: 1972. *Phonological Theory: Evolution and Current Practice*. ed. V. B. MAKKAI. N.Y.: Holt, Rinehart and Winston, Inc., pp. 153-165. Reprinted: 1973. *Phonology: Selected Writings*. ed. E. C. FUDGE. Middlesex, England: Penguin Books, pp. 115-135.

2.1.17 [and PIKE, EUNICE V.]: "Immediate Constituents of Mazatec Syllables." *International Journal of American Linguistics* 13(1947).78-91. Reprinted: 1975. *Studies in Tone and Intonation*. ed. RUTH M. BREND. Basel: S. Karger, pp. 62-83.

2.2.18 "Problems in the Teaching of Practical Phonemics." *Language Learning* 1(1948).3-8.

2.2.19 [and SINCLAIR, DONALD]: "The Tonemes of Mezquital Otomí." *International Journal of American Linguistics* 14(1948).91-98.

2.2.20 "Cuento Mixteco de un Conejo, un Coyote, y la Luna." *Revista Mexicana de Estudios Anthropológicos* 10(1948-49).133-134.

2.1.21 [and FRIES, CHARLES C.]: "Coexistent Phonemic Systems." *Language* 25(1949).25-50. Reprinted: 1972. *Kenneth L. Pike: Selected Writings,* pp. 51-73.

2.1.22 "A Problem in Morphology-Syntax Division." *Acta Linguistica,* pp. 74-84.

2.1.23 *Bibliography of the Summer Institute of Linguistics.* Glendale [now Huntington Beach], Calif.: Summer Institute of Linguistics, 1951.

2.1.24 "The Problems of Unwritten Languages in Education." Report in the UNESCO meeting of Experts in the Use of the Vernacular Languages. Paris: UNESCO, 1951, 27 pp.

2.1.25 "More on Grammatical Prerequisites." *Word* 8(1952).106-121. Reprinted: 1972. *Phonological Theory: Evolution and Current Practice,* ed. VALERIE BECKER MAKKAI. N.Y.: Holt, Rinehart and Winston, Inc., pp. 211-223.

2.1.26 "Operational Phonemics in Reference to Linguistic Relativity." *Journal of the Acoustical Society of America* 24(1952).618-625. Reprinted: 1972. *Kenneth L. Pike: Selected Writings,* pp. 85-99.

2.1.27 "Intonational Analysis of a Rumanian Sentence." *Cahiers Sextil Puşcariu* 2. University of Washington, Seattle, Dept. of Romance Languages and Literature, 1953, pp. 59-60.

2.1.28 "A Note on Allomorph Classes and Tonal Technique." *International Journal of American Lingusitics* 19(1953).101-105.

2.1.29 "Meaning and Hypostasis." *Monograph* 8. Georgetown University, Institute of Languages and Linguistics, 1955, 134-141.

2.1.30 [and PIKE, EUNICE V.]: *Live Issues in Descriptive Linguistics.* Santa Ana [now Huntington Beach], Calif.: Summer Institute of Linguistics. 2nd ed. 1960, iv + 41 pp.

2.1.31 "As Correntes da Linguistica Norteamericana." *Revista Brasileira de Filologia* 2(1956).207-216.

2.1.32 [and KINDBERG, WILLARD]: "A Problem in Multiple Stresses." *Word* 12(1956).415-428. Reprinted: 1975. *Studies in Tone and Intonation.* ed. RUTH M. BREND. Basel: S. Karger, pp. 212-226.

2.1.33 "Toward a Theory of the Structure of Human Behavior." *Estudios Anthropológicos Publicados en Homenaje al Doctor Manuel Gamio.* Mexico, D.F., 1956, pp. 659-671.

2.1.34 "Grammemic Theory in Reference to Restricted Problems of Morpheme Classes." *International Journal of American Linguistics* 23(1957). 119-128.

2.1.35 "Grammatical Theory." *General Linguistics* 2(1957).35-41.

2.1.36 [and BEASLEY, DAVID]: "Notes on Huambisa Phonemics." *Lingua Posnaniensis* 6(1957).1-8.

2.1.37 "Abdominal Pulse Types in Some Peruvian Languages." *Language* 33(1957).30-35. Reprinted: 1975. *Studies in Tone and Intonation,* ed. RUTH M. BREND. Basel: S. Karger, pp. 204-211.

2.1.38 "Language and Life: A Training Device for Translation and Practice." *Bibliotheca Sacra* 114(1957).347-362. Reprinted: 1972. *Kenneth L. Pike: Selected Writings,* pp. 117-128.

2.1.39 [and MATTESON, ESTHER]: "Non-Phonemic Transition Vocoids in Piro (Arawak)." *Miscellanea Phonetica* 3(1958).22-30.

2.1.40 "Interpenetration of Phonology, Morphology, and Syntax." *Proceedings of the Eighth International Congress of Linguists.* Oslo: University Press, 1958, pp. 363-374.

2.1.41 "On Tagmemes, *née* Gramemes." *International Journal of American Linguistics* 24(1958).273-278.

2.1.42 [and SAINT, RACHEL]: "Notas sobre Fonémica Huaraní (Auca)." *Estudios Acerca de las Lenguas Huaraní (Auca), Shimigae y Zápara: Publicaciones Científicas de Ministerio de Educación del Ecuador,* 1958, pp. 4-17.

2.1.43 [and BARRETT, RALPH P.; and BASCOM, BURT]: "Instrumental Collaboration on a Tepehuan (Uto-Aztecan) Pitch Problem." *Phonetica* 3(1959).1-22.

2.1.44 "Language as Particle, Wave, and Field." *The Texas Quarterly* 2 (1959).37-54. Reprinted: 1972. *Kenneth L. Pike: Selected Writings,* pp. 129-143.

2.1.45 "Linguistic Research as Pedagogical Support." *Papers of the National Conference on the Teaching of African Languages and Area Studies,* ed. JOHN G. BRODER. Georgetown University, 1960, pp. 32-39.

2.1.46 "Toward a Theory of Change and Bilingualism." *Studies in Linguistics* 15(1960).1-7.

2.1.47 "Nucleation." *The Modern Language Journal* 44(1960).291-295. Reprinted: ILT *News* [Journal of the Institute of Language Teaching, Waseda University, Tokyo] 6(1961).1-5. Reprinted: *Philippine Journal for Language Teaching* 1(1963).1-7, 20. Reprinted: *Teaching English as a Second Language*, ed. HAROLD B. ALLEN. N.Y.: McGraw-Hill, 1965, pp. 67-74. Reprinted: *Kenneth L. Pike: Selected Writings*, pp. 144-150.

2.1.48 "Building Sympathy." *Practical Anthropology* 7(1960).250-252.

2.1.49 "Stimulating and Resisting Change." *Practical Anthropology* 8(1961).267-274.

2.1.50 "Compound Affixes in Ocaina." *Language* 37(1961).570-581.

2.1.51 [and WARKENTIN, MILTON]: "Huave: A Study in Syntactic Tone with Low Lexical Functional Load." *A William Cameron Townsend en el Vigesimoquinto Aniversario del Instituto Lingüístico de Verano.* Mexico, D.F.: Instituto Lingüístico de Verano, 1961, pp. 627-642.

2.1.52 [and SAINT, RACHEL]: "Auca Phonemes." *Studies in Ecuadorian Indian Languages* I. Norman, Okla.: Summer Institute of Linguistics and the University of Oklahoma, 1962, pp. 2-30.

2.1.53 "Practical Phonetics of Rhythm Waves." *Phonetica* 8(1962).9-30. Reprinted: *Studies in Tone and Intonation*, ed. RUTH M. BREND, Basel: S. Karger, 1962, pp. 11-32.

2.1.54 "Dimensions of Grammatical Constructions." *Language* 38(1962). 221-244. Reprinted: *Kenneth L. Pike: Selected Writings*, pp. 160-185.

2.1.55 [and SCOTT, GRAHAM]: "Pitch Accent and Non-Accented Phrases in Fore (New Guinea)." *Zeitschrift für Phonetik, Sprachwissenschaft und Kommunikationsforschung* 16(1963).179-189.

2.1.56 "Choices in Course Design." *The Teaching of Linguistics in Anthropology.* Memoir 94, American Anthropological Association, 1963, pp. 315-332.

2.1.57 "Theoretical Implications of Matrix Permutation in Fore (New Guinea)." *Anthropological Linguistics* 5:8(1963).1-23.

2.1.58 "A Syntactic Paradigm." *Language* 39(1963)216-230. Reprinted: *Advances in Tagmemics*, ed. RUTH M. BREND. Amsterdam: North-Holland Publishing Co., 1963, pp. 235-249.

2.1.59 "The Hierarchical and Social Matrix of Suprasegmentals." *Prace Filologiczne* 18(1963).95-104.

2.1.60 "A Linguistic Contribution to Composition: A Hypothesis." *Journal of the Conference on College Composition and Communication,* 15(1964).82-88.

2.1.61 [and LARSON, MILDRED]: "Hyperphonemes and Non-Systematic Features of Aguaruna Phonemics." *Studies in Languages and Linguistics in Honor of Charles C. Fries,* ed. A. H. MARCKWARDT. Ann Arbor: The English Language Institute of the University of Michigan, 1964, pp. 55-67.

2.1.62 [and ERICKSON, BARBARA]: "Conflated Field Structures in Potawatomi and in Arabic." *International Journal of American Linguistics* 30 (1964).201-212. Reprinted: *Advances in Tagmemics,* ed. RUTH M. BREND. Amsterdam: North-Holland Publishing Co., 1964, pp. 135-146.

2.1.63 "Beyond the Sentence." *Journal of the Conference on College Composition and Communication* 15(1964).129-135. Reprinted 1972, *Kenneth L. Pike: Selected Writings,* pp. 192-199.

2.1.64 "Discourse Analysis and Tagmeme Matrices." *Oceanic Linguistics* 3(1964).5-25. Reprinted: *Advances in Tagmemics,* ed. RUTH M. BREND. Amsterdam: North-Holland Publishing Co., 1974, pp. 285-305.

2.1.65 [and BECKER, ALTON]: "Progressive Neutralization in Dimensions of Navaho Stem Matrices." *International Journal of American Linguistics* 30 (1964).144-145.

2.1.66 "Stress Trains in Auca." *In Honour of Daniel Jones,* ed. D. ABERCROMBIE; D. B. FRY; A. C. MACCARTHY; N. C. SCOTT; and J. L. M. TRIM. London: Longmans, Green, 1964, pp. 425-431. Reprinted: 1972. *Kenneth L. Pike: Selected Writings,* pp. 186-191.

2.1.67 "Name Fusions as High-Level Particles in Matrix Theory." *Linguistics* 6(1964).83-91.

2.1.68 "On Systems of Grammatical Structure." *Proceedings of the Ninth International Congress of Linguists.* ed. H. G. LUNT. The Hague: Mouton, 1964, pp. 145-154. Reprinted: 1972. *Kenneth L. Pike: Selected Writings,* pp. 200-208.

2.1.69 "Language—Where Science and Poetry Meet." *College English* 26(1965).283-292.

2.1.70 "Non-Linear Order and Anti-Redundancy in German Morphological Matrices." *Zeitschrift für Mundartforschung* 32(1965).193-221.

2.1.71 "A Guide to Publications Related to Tagmemic Theory." *Current Trends in Linguistics* 3. ed. T. A SEBEOK. The Hague: Mouton, 1966, pp. 365-394.

2.1.72 "On the Grammar of Intonation." *Proceedings of the Fifth International Congress of Phonetic Sciences.* ed. E. ZWIRNER and W. BETHGE. Basel: S. Karger, 1966, pp. 105-119. Reprinted: *Studies in Tone and Intonation,* ed. RUTH M. BREND. Basel: S. Karger, 1975, pp. 33-44.

2.1.73 "Suprasegmental in Reference to Phonemes of Item, of Process, and of Relation." *To Honor Roman Jakobson.* The Hague: Mouton, 1967, pp. 1545-1554. Reprinted: *Studies in Tone and Intonation,* ed. RUTH M. BREND. Basel: S. Karger, 1975, pp. 45-56.

2.1.74 "Tongue-Root Position in Practical Phonetics." *Phonetica* 17 (1967).129-140. Reprinted: 1972. *Kenneth L. Pike: Selected Writings,* pp. 221-230.

2.1.75 "Grammar as Wave." *Monograph* 20. Georgetown University, Institute of Languages and Linguistics, 1967, pp. 1-14. Reprinted: 1972. *Kenneth L. Pike: Selected Writings,* pp. 231-241.

2.1.76 "How to Make an Index." *Publications of the Modern Language Association of America* 83(1968).991-993.

2.1.77 [and JACOBS, GILL]: "Matrix Permutation as a Heuristic Device in the Analysis of the Bimoba Verb." *Lingua* 21(1968).321-345. Reprinted: 1972. *Kenneth L. Pike: Selected Writings,* pp. 242-262.

2.1.78 "Indirect Versus Direct Discourse in Bariba." *Proceedings of the Conference on Language and Language Behavior.* ed. M. ZALE. N.Y.: Appleton-Century-Crofts, 1968, pp. 165-173.

2.1.79 "Professor Charles C. Fries." *Language Learning* 18(1968).1-2.

2.1.80 "Language as Behavior and Etic and Emic Standpoints for the Description of Behavior." *Social Psychology: Readings and Perspective.* ed. E. F. BORGATTA. Chicago: Rand, McNally, 1969, pp. 114-131. Reprinted from *Language in Relation to a Unified Theory of the Structure of Human Behavior.*

2.1.81 [and LOWE, IVAN]: "Pronominal Reference in English Conversation and Discourse: A Group Theoretical Treatment." *Folia Linguistica* 3(1969). 68-106. Reprinted: 1972. *Kenneth L. Pike: Selected Writings,* pp. 263-297.

2.1.82 "The Role of Nuclei of Feet in the Analysis of Tone in Tibeto-Burman Languages of Nepal." *Prosodic Feature Analysis.* eds. LEON, and FAURE, and RIGAULT. *Studia Phonetica* 3(1970).153-161. Reprinted: 1970. *Tone Systems of Tibeto-Burman Languages of Nepal,* Part I. eds. AUSTIN HALE and KENNETH L. PIKE, pp. 37-48.

2.1.83 [and HARI, MARIA; and TAYLOR, DOREEN]: "Tamang Tone and Higher Levels." *Tone Systems of Tibeto-Burman Languages of Nepal,* Part I. eds. AUSTIN HALE and KENNETH L. PIKE, 1970, pp. 82-124.

2.1.84 "More Revolution: Tagmemics." Ch. 7 of *Reading About Language.* eds. C. LAIRD and R. M. GORRELL. N.Y.: Harcourt, Brace, Jovanovich, 1971, pp. 234-247.

2.1.85 "Implications of the Patterning of an Oral Reading of a Set of Poems." *Poetics* 1(1971).38-45.

2.1.86 "Crucial Questions in the Development of Tagmemics—the Sixties and the Seventies." *Monograph* 24, Georgetown University, Institute of Languages and Linguistics, 1971, pp. 79-98.

2.1.87 [and SCHOETTEINDREYER, BURKHARD]: "Paired-Sentence Reversals in the Discovery of Underlying and Surface Structures in Sherpa Discourse." *Indian Linguistics* 33:1(1972).72-83. Reprinted: 1973. *Clause, Sentence, and Discourse Patterns in Selected Languages of Nepal,* Part I. Summer Institute of Linguistic Publications in Linguistics and Related Fields, 40. ed. AUSTIN HALE, pp. 361-375.

2.1.88 [and GORDON, KENT]: "Preliminary Technology to Show Emic Relations Between Certain Non-Transitivity Clause Structures in Dhanger (Kudux, Nepal)." *International Journal of Dravidian Linguistics* 1:1(1972). 56-79

2.1.89 [and PIKE, EVELYN G.]: "Seven Substitution Exercise for Studying the Structure of Discourse.." *Linguistics* 94(1972).43-52.

2.1.90 "Comments on Gleason's 'Grammatical Prerequisites'." *Annals of the New York Academy of Sciences,* 211(1973).34-38.

2.1.91 [and SCHOETTEINDREYER, BURKHARD]: "Notation for Simultaneous Representation of Grammatical and Sememic Components in Connected

Discourse." *Clause, Sentence, and Discourse Patterns in Selected Languages of Nepal,* Part I. Summer Institute of Linguistics Publications in Linguistics and Related Fields 40. ed. AUSTIN HALE, 1973, pp. 321-360.

2.1.92 [and GORDON, KENT H.]: "Paired Semantic Components, Paired Sentence Reversals and the Analysis of Dhanger (Kudux) Discourse." *International Journal of Dravidian Linguistics* 2:1(1973).14-46. Reprinted: 1973. *Patterns in Clause, Sentence, and Discourse in Selected Languages of Nepal.* Part I. Summer Institute of Linguistics Publications in Linguistics and Related Fields 41. ed. RONALD L. TRAIL, 1973, 313-343.

2.1.93 "Sociolinguistic Evaluation of Alternative Mathematical Models: English Pronouns." *Language* 49(1973).121-160.

2.1.94 "Science Fiction ᵤₛ a Test of Axioms Concerning Human Behavior." *Parma Eldalamberon* 1:3(1973).3-4.

2.1.95 "Agreement Types Dispersed into a Nine-Cell Spectrum." *On Language, Culture, and Religion: In Honor of Eugene A. Nida,* eds. MATTHEW BLACK and WILLIAM A. SMALLEY. The Hague: Mouton, 1974, pp. 275-286.

2.1.96 "Recent Developments in Tagmemics." *Proceedings of the Eleventh International Congress of Linguists, Bologna-Florence, 1972.* Vol. I. ed. LUIGI HEILMANN. Bologna: Mulino, 1974, pp. 163-172. Reprinted: *Linguistics at the Crossroads.* eds. ADAM MAKKAI, VALERIE BECKER MAKKAI, LUIGI HEILMANN. Lake Bluff, Ill.: Jupiter Press, 1974, pp. 155-166.

2.1.97 [and PIKE, EVELYN G.]: "Rules as Components of Tagmemes in the English Verb Phrase." *Advances in Tagmemics.* ed. RUTH M. BREND. Amsterdam: North-Holland Publishing Co., 1974, pp. 175-204.

2.1.98 [and MARTIN, R.]: "Analysis of the Vocal Performance of a Poem: A Classification of Intonational Features." *Language and Style* 7(1974). 209-218.

2.1.99 "Focus in English Clause Structure Seen Via Systematic Experimental Syntax." *Kivung* 8(1975).3-14.

2.1.100 "On Describing Languages." *The Scope of American Linguistics.* ed. ROBERT AUSTERLITZ. Lisse, The Netherlands: The Peter de Ridder Press, 1975, pp. 9-39.

2.1.101 "On Kinesic Triadic Relations in Turn-Taking." *Semiotica* 13 (1975).389-394.

2.1.102 [and STERNER, ROBERT; and SUHARNO, IGNATIUS]: "Experimental Syntax Applied to the Relation Between Sentence and Sentence Cluster in Indonesian." *From Baudi to Indonesian,* 1976, pp. 95-117.

2.1.103 "Pike's Answers to 12 Questions for Conference on Language Universals." held at Gummersbach, October 4-8, 1976. In *Materials for the DFG International Conference on Language Universals,* AKUP (Arbeiten des Kölner Universalien-Projekts) 25(1976).170-176.

2.1.104 [and PIKE, EVELYN G.]: "The Granular Nature of a Construction as Illustrated by 'Flying Planes'." *From Baudi to Indonesian,* 1976, pp. 29-37.

2.1.105 "The Meaning of Particles in Text: A Random Note." *From Baudi to Indonesian,* 1976, pp. 41-44.

2.1.106 "Toward the Development of Tagmemic Postulates." in *Tagmemics: Theoretical Discourse.* Vol. II. The Hague: Mouton, 1976, pp. 91-127.

2.1.107 [and HUTTAR, GEORGE L.]: "How Many Packages?" *Hemisphere* 21:12(1977).26-29.

2.1.108 [and PIKE, EVELYN G.]: "Referential Versus Grammatical Hierarchies." *The Third Lacus Forum* 1976. eds. ROBERT J. DIPIETRO and EDWARD L. BLANSITT, JR. Columbia, South Carolina: Hornbeam Press, 1977, pp. 343-354.

2.1.109 (ed.) *Pilot Projects on the Reading of English of Science and Technology.* University of Michigan Papers in Linguistics Special Publications in Applied Linguistics, 1. Ann Arbor: Department of Linguistics, University of Michigan, 1977.

2.1.110 "Introduction: On the Relation Between Modes of Argumentation in Linguistic Analysis Versus the Documentation of Change of Behavior in Reading." *Pilot Projects on the Reading of English of Science and Technology.* ed. KENNETH L. PIKE. Ann Arbor: Department of Linguistics, University of Michigan, 1977, pp. 1-5.

2.1.111 [and BERNSTEIN, JARED]: "The Emic Structure of Individuals in Relation to Dialogue." Grammars and Descriptions, eds. TEUN A. VAN DIJK and JÁNOS S. PETÖFI. Berlin: Gruyter, 1977, pp. 1-10.

2.1.112 "Particularization Versus Generalization, and Explanation Versus Prediction." *The Teaching of English in Japan,* eds. IKUO KOIKE, MASUO MATSOYAMA, YASUO IGARASHI, and KOKI SUZUKI. Tokyo: Eichosah Publishing Co., Ltd., 1978, pp. 783-785.

2.1.113 "Thresholdism Versus Reductionism." *Language Universals.* ed. HANSJAKOB SEILER. Tübingen: Gunter Narr Verlag, 1978, pp. 53-58.

2.1.114 "Social Interaction as the Break-in Point for the Analysis of Verbal Behavior." *Proceedings of the Twelfth International Congress of Linguists, Vienna, August 28-September 2, 1977,* (1978).739-741.

2.1.115 "Linguistics—From There to Where?" *The Fifth Lacus Forum 1978.* eds. WOLFGANG WÖLCK and PAUL L. GARVIN. Columbia, South Carolina: Hornbeam Press, 1979, pp. 3-18.

2.1.116 "Universals and Phonetic Hierarchy." In: *Proceedings of the Ninth International Congress of Phonetic Sciences, Copenhagen, August 6-11, 1979.* eds. ELI FISCHER-JORGENSEN, JORGEN RISCHEL, and NINA THORSEN, 1979, pp. 48-52.

2.1.117 "Social Linguistics and Bilingual Education." *System* 7(1979). 99-109.

2.1.118 "On the Extension of Etic-Emic Anthropological Methodology to Referential Units-in-Context." *Lembaran Tengkajian Budaya* 3(1979).1-36.

2.1.119 "Notes on the Academic Programme of the Summer Institute of Linguistics Around the World." *Sabah Museum Annals* 1(1979).1-12.

2.1.120 "A Note of Some Universals of Human Behaviour." *Sabah Museum Annals* 1(1979).47-55.

2.1.121 [and DuBOIS, CARL D.; and UPTON, JOHN]: "Constraints on Complexity Seen via Fused Vectors of an n-Dimensional Semantic Space (Sarangani, Manobo, Philippines)." *Semiotica* 29:3-4(1980).209-243.

2.1.122 "Here We Stand—Creative Observers of Language." *Approches du Langage: Colloque Interdisciplinaire.* eds. REUCHLIN and FRANÇOIS. Publications de la Sorbonne, Série "Études" 16(1980).9-45.

2.1.123 "Wherein Lies 'Talked-About' Reality?" *A Festschrift for Native Speaker.* ed. FLORIAN COULMAS. The Hague: Mouton, 1981, pp. 85-91.

2.1.124 "Systematic Planned Distortion of Text as a Clue to Translation Problems: A Query." *Suniti Chatterji Commemoration Volume,* ed. BHAKTAI PRASAD MALLIK. West Bengal, India: The University of Burdwan, 1981, pp. 163-166.

2.1.125 "An Autobiographical Note on Phonetics." *Towards a History of Phonetics.* ed. R. E. ASHER and EUGINIE J. A. HENDERSON. Edinburgh: The University Press, 1981, pp. 181-185.

2.1.126 "Dreams of an Integrated Theory of Experience." *Waiyu Jiaoxue Yu Yanjiu* [Foreign Language Teaching and Research] 1(1981).24-33, 12.

2.1.127 "Nonsense in the Service of Sense." *Language and Communication* 1(1981).179-188.

2.1.128 "Some Questions for Field Linguists Beginning Language Analysis." *Notes on Linguistics* 24(1982).3-14.

2.1.129 [and SOUTAR, JEAN]: "Texts Illustrating the Analysis of Direct versus Indirect Quotations in Bariba." *Language Data, Africa Data 19* (Microfiche, 312 frames). Dallas: Summer Institute of Linguistics, 1982.

2.1.130 "Tune and Tone: Generalized Syntagmatic Pitch Patterns Constrained by Particular Lexical Patterns." *Journal of West African Languages* 12:2(1982).22-41.

2.1.131 "Phonological Hierarchy in a Four-Cell Tagmemic Representation from Discourse to Phoneme Class." *Forum Linguisticum* 7(1982).65-91.

2.1.132 "In Rhetoric the Passage from A to B i Not Equal to Passage from B to A." *Work papers of the Summer Institute of Linguistics, University of North Dakota.* 27(1983).135-137.

2.1.133 "Experimental Syntax: A Basis for Some New Language-Learning Exercises." *Arab Journal of Language Studies* 1:2(1983).245-255.

2.1.134 "On Understanding People: An Integrative Philosophy." *The Ninth LACUS Forum 1982.* ed. JOHN MORREALL. Columbia, South Carolina: Hornbeam Press, 1983, pp. 129-136.

2.1.135 "Universal Terms as Waves." *Essays in Honor of Charles F. Hockett.* eds. FREDERICK B. AGARD and GERALD KELLEY. Leiden: E. J. Brill, 1983, pp. 126-127.

2.1.136 "Grammar versus Reference in the Analysis of Discourse." *Perspectives dans l'analyse du discours.* ed. THOMAS BEARTH. Abidjan, Ivory Coast: Institut de Linguistique Applique, 1983, pp. 23-42.

2.1.137 "The Future for Unit-in-Context: The Tagmeme." *Proceedings of the XIIIth International Congress of Linguists, 1982.* Tokyo, 1983, pp. 881-883.

2.1.138 "Quelques suggestions pour les premiers stages d'une analyse linguistique." *Études Linguistiques Preliminaires Dans Quelques Langues Du Togo.* ed. JACQUES NICOLE. Lome, Togo: Société Internationale de Linguistique, 1983, pp. 8-17.

2.1.139 "The Translator's Voice: An Interview with Kenneth Pike." An interview by Elizabeth Miller. *Translation Review,* University of Texas at Dallas, 12(1983).1-10.

2.1.140 [and KAREN, MARK E.]: "Notes on Phonological Grouping in Kalenjin (Kenya) in Relation to Tone, Intonation Patterns, and Vowel Harmony." *Occasional Papers in the Study of Sudanese Languages* 3(1984). 47-59.

2.1.141 "Some Teachers Who Helped Me." *Historiographia Linguistica* 11(1984).493-495.

2.1.142 "Assumptions in Maxwell's Article 'The Generative Revolution and the Summer Institute of Linguistics'." *Notes on Linguistics* 29(1984).48-50..

2.1.143 [and BARBARA KELLER]: "The Integration of Self in Society Through Language." *AILA Brussels 84, Proceedings,* (7th World Congress of Applied Linguistics) 5(1984).1877-1900.

2.1.144 "The Need for Rejection of Autonomy in Linguistics." *The Eleventh LACUS Forum 1984.* Columbia, South Carolina: Hornbeam Press, 1985, pp. 35-53.

2.1.145 "Language, Linguistics and Linguists: A Panel Discussion, with Gregory et al." *Langues et linguistique* 11(1985).1-36.

2.1.146 "Systemic Emic Pattern above Abstract Etic Universals—*A Query.*" *Word* 36(1985).179-181.

2.1.147 "Static, Dynamic, and Relational Perspectives Suggested in Words and Phrases." *Scientific and Humanistic Dimensions of Language, Festschrift for Robert Lado.* ed. KURT R. JANKOWSKY. Amsterdam/Philadelphia: J. Benjamins, 1985, pp. 447-452.

2.1.148 [and FRIES, PETER H.]: "Slot and Referential Hierarchy in Relation to Charles C. Fries' View of Language." *Toward an Understanding of Language: Charles C. Fries in Perspective,* eds. PETER HOWARD FRIES, et al. Amsterdam/Philadelphia: J. Benjamins, 1985, pp. 105-127.

2.1.149 "Mixtec Social 'Credit Rating' – The Particular Versus the Universal in One Emic World View." *Proceedings of the National Academy of Sciences of the United States of America*, 83(1986)3047-3049.

2.1.150 "On the Value of Local Languages." *Languages in the International Perspective*. ed. NANCY SCHWEDA-NICHOLSON. Delaware Symposium 5 (1986).13-19.

2.1.151 "A Further Note On Experimental Clauses in Discourse." *Language in Global Perspective: Papers in Honˑr of the 50th Anniversary of the Summer Institute of Linguistics 1935-1985*. ed. BENJAMIN ELSON. Dallas: Summer Institute of Linguistics, 1986, pp. 135-138.

2.2 Religion

2.2.1 *God's Guidance and Your Life's Work*. Chicago: Inter-Varsity Christian Fellowship, 1947. Reprinted: 1955 by Wycliffe Bible Translators, Santa Ana [now Huntington Beach], Calif.

2.2.2 "Living on Manna." *The Sunday School Times* May 1, 1951, pp. 3-4.

2.2.3 "We'll Tell Them, But in What Language?" *His* 12:2(1951).8-11, 14.

2.2.4 "Gold, Frankincense, and Myrrh." *The King's Business* 42:12 (1957).16-17.

2.2.5 "Why I Believe in God." *His* 18:2(1957).3-7, 32-33.

2.2.6 "Prescription for Intellectuals." *Eternity* 8:8(1957).11, 44-45.

2.2.7 "A Stereoscope Window on the World." *Bibliotheca Sacra* 114 (1957).141-156.

2.2.8 "Slots and Classes in the Hierarchical Structure of Behavior." *Bibliotheca Sacra* 114(1957).255-262.

2.2.9 "A Training Device for Translation Theory and Practice." *Bibliotheca Sacra* 114(1957).347-362.

2.2.10 "Tristructural Units of Human Behavior." *Bibliotheca Sacra* 115 (1958).36-43.

2.2.11 *Language and Life*. The four preceding articles reprinted from *Bibliotheca Sacra*, 1958.

2.2.12 "Serving our Colleagues." *His* 18:5(1958).5-7.

2.2.13 "The Sin of Independence." *His* 18:8(1958).5-7.

2.2.14 "The Individual." *Eternity* 9:9(1958).18-19.

2.2.15 "Marriage." mimeograph, 1959.

2.2.16 "Our Own Tongue Wherein We Were Born: The Work of the Summer Institute of Linguistics and the Wycliffe Bible Translators." *The Bible Translator* 10:2(1959).3-15.

2.2.17 "Intellectual Idolatry." *His* 19:5(1959).5-6.

2.2.18 "Walking." *The King's Business* 50:4(1959).10-11.

2.2.19 "A Linguistic Parable." *His* 19:6(1959).39-40.

2.2.20 "Why the Angels Are Curious." *The King's Business* 50:9(1959).12-13.

2.2.21 "Cause-and-Effect in the Christian Life." *His* 20:1(1959).33-34.

2.2.22 "Players." *His* 20:9(1960).41-42.

2.2.23 "When Failure is Success." *The Alliance Witness* 95:21(1960).5.

2.2.24 "Why There is a Moral Code." *The King's Business* 51:10(1960).10-11.

2.2.25 "Strange Dimensions of Truth." *Christianity Today* 5(1961).690-692. Reprinted: 1972. *Kenneth L. Pike: Selected Writings*, pp. 301-306.

2.2.26 "Current Strategy in Missions." *His* 22:9(1961).13-14.

2.2.27 "Left-Handed." *His* 22:9(1962).36-47.

2.2.28 "Modern Christianity's Crucial Junctures [a note in a list of comments by scholars]." *Christianity Today* 8:1(1963).32.

2.2.29 "Man or Robot." *Eternity* 15:2(1964).9-11, 46.

2.2.30 "Christianity and Science." *The Church Herald* 22:4(1965).4-6.

2.2.31 "Tempted to Quit." *The Church Herald* 23:6(1966).14-26. Reprinted: *The Christian Athlete,* (Feb., 1966):11.

2.2.32 "The Disillusioned Scholar." *The Church Herald* 23:30(1966). 15, 30.

2.2.33 "God in History." *The Church Herald* 23:2(1966).4-5, 22.

2.2.34 "The Courage to Face Tension." *The Church Herald* 24:21(1967).11.

2.2.35 "Abraham My Father." *The Alliance Witness* 102:25(1967).9, 19.

2.2.36 "Intergenerational Cleavage." *Translation* (Jan.-Feb., 1968).4-5.

2.2.37 Review of *You! Jonah!* (by J. T. Carlisle). *Christianity Today* 13:2(1968)22-23.

2.2.38 "Mental Tension." *The King's Business* 58:2(1968).30-31.

2.2.39 "Mission and Social Concern [a letter to the editor]." *His* 28 (March, 1968).26.

2.2.40 "Termites and Eternity." *His* 28:7(1968)4-5.

2.2.41 "Guest editorial: On Finding God's Role for You." *Missionary Messenger* (organ of the Eastern Mennonite Board of Missions and Charities) 45:8(1969).23-24.

2.2.42 "Good Out of a Student Strike [a letter to the editor]." *The Church Herald* 27:18(1970).17.

2.2.43 "The Linguist and Axioms Concerning Language of Scripture." *Interchange* 3:2(1971).77-84. Reprinted in *Journal of the American Scientific Affiliation* 26(1974).47-51.

2.2.44 "Language." *Christ and the Modern Mind.* Ed. ROBERT W. SMITH. Downers Grove, Ill.: Inter-Varsity Press, 1972, pp. 59-67.

2.2.45 "Language and Faith." *Language and Faith.* Santa Ana [now Huntington Beach], Calif.: Wycliffe Bible Translators, 1972, pp. 18-30.

2.2.46 "Morals and Metaphor." *Interchange* 12(1972).228-231.

2.2.47 *Use What You Have* (Six cassette tapes, twelve religious talks, published as a set). Costa Mesa, Calif.: One Way Library, 1972.

2.2.48 "[Jesus Choosing His Disciples]" in Seed Thoughts, *His* 34:2 (1973).7.

2.2.49 "Language and Self Image." *The Scientist and Ethical Decision.* ed. CHARLES HATFIELD. Downers Grove, Ill.: Inter-Varsity Press, 1973, pp. 69-82.

2.2.50 "[The Sluggard]" in Seed Thoughts, *His* 34:4(1974).13.

2.2.51 "[A Chain Reaction]" in Seed Thoughts, *His* 34:6(1974).22.

2.2.52 "[Attacked — Nehemiah]" in Seed Thoughts, *His* 34:8(1974).4.

2.2.53 "[Flagellation]" in Seed Thoughts, *His* 34:9(1974).21.

2.2.54 "[God Remembers Us By Name]" in Seed Thoughts, *His* 35:1 (1974).23.

2.2.55 "[Power When We're Weak]" in Seed Thoughts, *His* 35:3(1974).23.

2.2.56 "The Linguist and Axioms Concerning Language of Scripture." *Journal of the American Scientific Affiliation* 26(1974).47-51. Reprinted from *Interchange* 3:2(1971).77-84.

2.2.57 "Analogies to the Good News." (Review: 1974 *Peace Child* by Don Richardson.) *Christianity Today* 20(Oct., 1975).91-92. A different review, also of *Peace Child* in *His* 36:5(1975).26.

2.2.58 "[In the Interest of Others — Diotrephes]" in Seed Thoughts, *His* 35:5(1975).21.

2.2.59 "[Jacob Valued the Birthright]" in Seed Thoughts, *His* 35:7 (1975).27.

2.2.60 "[A Spiritual Democracy — Korah]" in Seed Thoughts, *His* 35:8 (1975).5.

2.2.61 "[Two Timid Men — Joseph of Arimathea and Nicodemus]" in Seed Thoughts, *His* 35:9(1975).12.

2.2.62 "[An Unforgiving Spirit — Ahithophel]" in Seed Thoughts, *His* 36:1(1975).26.

2.2.63 Review of *Naked and Not Ashamed*, by LOWELL L. NOBEL. *Christianity Today* 21:4(1976).42.

2.2.64 "A Mighty Coral Reef" in Seed Thoughts, *His* 36:8(1976).7.

2.2.65 "How to Sin Righteously—[Balaam]" in Seed Thoughts, *His* 36:9(1976).22.

2.2.66 "Well Worth Doing" in Seed Thoughts, *His* 37:2(1976).8.

2.2.67 "[Serving One Another]" in Seed Thoughts, *His* 37:4(1977).31.

2.2.68 "[The Excuse Is Gone]" in Seed Thoughts, *His* 37:6(1977).15.

2.2.69 "[Practical Advice in Marriage]" in Seed Thoughts, *His* 37:7 (1977).9.

2.2.70 "Truth and Responsibility—[Pilate]" in Seed Thoughts, *His* 39:5 (1979).13.

2.2.71 "Love God with Mind—and Bless Babylon." *The Gordon Alumnus* 8:4(1979).6-7.

2.2.72 "Christianity and Culture I. Conscience and Culture." *Journal of the American Scientific Affiliation* 31(1979).8-12.

2.2.73 "Christianity and Culture II. Incarnation in a Culture." *Journal of the American Scientific Affiliation* 31(1979).92-96.

2.2.74 "Christianity and Culture III. Biblical Absolutes and Certain Cultural Relativisms." *Journal of the American Scientific Affiliation* 31(1979). 139-145.

2.2.75 "Emotion in God, and its Image in Us." *The Banner* 114:45 (1979).4-5.

2.2.76 "Intellectual Initiative: the Image of God." *The Banner* 114 (1979).10.

2.2.77 "An Image of His Debating Technique." *The Banner* 115:14 (1980).6-7.

2.2.78 "Servants." *Stillpoint* 2:1(1986).8. Wenham, Massachusetts: Gordon College.

2.3 Poetics

2.3.1 "Flaming Candle." *His* 18:7(1958).30.

2.3.2 "Crushed." *Translation.* Spring, 1966, p. 12. Reprinted: *Stir-Change-Create.* KENNETH L. PIKE. Grand Rapids, Mich.: Wm. B. Eerdmans, 1967, p. 109.

2.3.3 "In War—or Fuss." *Overflow* 2:1(1968).16.

2.3.4 "The Day Before Christmas." *Overflow* 2:1(1968).8.

2.3.5 "Fear." (two poems), *His* 29:9(1969).13.

2.3.6 "Five Poems." *Essays in Honor of Claude M. Wise.* eds. A. J. BRONSTEIN; C. L. SHAVER; and G. STEVENS. Hannibal, Mo.: The Standard Printing Co., 1970, pp. 67-72.

2.3.7 "Implications of the Patterning of an Oral Reading of a Set of Poems." *Poetics* 1(1971).38-45.

2.3.8 "Don't Jitter." *The Forum,* 1974, p. 14.

2.3.9 "New Year's Resolutions." *The Forum,* 1974, p. 13.

2.3.10 [and MARTIN, HOWARD R.]: "Analysis of the Vocal Performance of a Poem: A Classification of Intonational Features." *Language and Style* 7(1974).209-218.

2.3.11 "A Poem on Disconnecting Form and Meaning." *Linguistic and Literary Studies in Honor of Archibald A. Hill: Vol. I General and Theoretical Linguistics.* eds. MOHAMMAD ALI JAZAYERY, EDGAR C. POLOMÉ, WERNER WINTER. Lisse, The Netherlands: The Peter de Ridder Press, 1976, pp. 233-234.

2.3.12 [Ten Poems, reprinted]. *Linguistic Muse.* eds. DONNA JO NAPOLI and EMILY N. RANDO. Carbondale: Linguistic Research Inc., 1979, pp. 138-144.

2.3.13 "Towards the Linguistic Analysis of One's Own Poems." *The Tenth LACUS Forum 1983.* Columbia, S.C.: Hornbeam Press, 1984, pp. 117-128.

2.3.14 "Person Above Logic." *New Perspectives in Language, Culture and Personality: Proceedings of the Edward Sapir Centenary Conference.* eds. WILLIAM COWAN, MICHAEL K. FOSTER and KONRAD KOERNER. Amsterdam, (in press).

(See also *Stir-Change-Create, Mark My Words,* and *Songs of Fun and Faith,* listed under Religion.)

3. EDUCATIONAL TELEVISION PROGRAMS

Pike on Language, series. On ¾ inch videocassettes (NTSC standard) and on 16mm kinescopes. Ann Arbor: University of Michigan Television Center, The University of Michigan, 1977.

Program No. 1: "Voices at Work [Phonetics]"
Program No. 2: "The Music of Speech [Pitch and Poetry]"
Program No. 3: "Waves of Change [The How and Why of Change in Language]"
Program No. 4: "The Way We Know – The Value of Theory in Linguistic Study"
Program No. 5: "Into the Unknown [Learning an Unknown Language by Gesture – a Monolingual Demonstration]"

4. REVIEWS OF KENNETH LEE PIKE'S BOOKS
(A Partial Listing)

4.1 **Pronunciation** (1942)

WONDERLY, W. L.: *International Journal of American Linguistics* 14(1948).60.

4.2 **Phonetics** (1943)

The Draftsman, 37 (1943).
TRAGER, G. L.: *Studies in Linguistics* 2(1943).16-20.
DE LATTRE, P.: *Books Abroad* 18(1944).384-385.
HOENIGSWALD, H.: *Journal of the American Oriental Society* 64 (1944).151-155.
MCDAVID, RAVEN: *South Central Bulletin* 4(1944).6.
THOMAS, C. K.: *American Speech* 19(1944).54-55.
TRAGER, G. L.: *Journal of English and German Philology* 43(1944). 101-102.
FLOREZ, L.: *Boletin del Instituto Caro y Cueva* 1(1945).179-180.
FISCHER-JØRGENSEN, ELI: *Acta Linguistica Hafniensis* 5(1945-49). 42-43.
EMMENEAU, M.: *American Journal of Philology* 67(1946).92-94.
MARTINET, ANDRÉ: *Bulletin de la Societé de Linguistique de Paris* (1947).29-31.
STURTEVANT, E.: *Studies in Linguistics* 5(1947).33-42.
PRESTON, W. D.: *American Anthropologist* 50(1948).127-128.
FISCHER-JØRGENSEN, ELI: *Journal of English Letters and Philology* 31(1950).67-70.
VINAY, J. P.: *Le Maître Phonetique* 3:93(1950).14-17.

4.3 **The Intonation of American English** (1945).
BOLINGER, D. L.: *American Speech* 22(1947).134-146.
HENDERSON, E.: *Modern Language Review* 42(1947).542.
PENZL, H.: *Journal of English and German Philology* 46(1947).
140-142.
WELLS, RULON: *Language* 23(1947).255-273.
ABERCROMBIE, D.: *Review of English Studies* 25(1969).369-370.
FISCHER-JØRGENSEN, ELI: *Lingua* 2(1949).3-13.
PREPRNIK: *Philologica* 5(1949).9-11.
LEE: *Casopis pro Moderni Filogii* 33(1949-50).61-64.

4.4 **Phonemics** (1947).
FISCHER-JØRGENSEN, ELI: *Acta Linguistica Academiae Scientiarum Hungaricae* 5(1945-49).104-109.
THOMAS, C. K.: *Quarterly Journal of Speech* 34(1948).384.
WONDERLY, W. L.: *International Journal of American Linguistics* 14(1948).60.
BOLDESEN, C. A.: *English Studies* (Amsterdam), 30(1949).26-27.
ECHOLS, J. M.: *Journal of English and German Philology* 48(1949).
377-379.
HAUGEN, EINAR: *American Speech* 24(1949).54-57.
HOCKETT, C.: *Studies in Linguistics* 7(1949).49-51.
VALENCIA, A.: *Boletin del Instituto Caro y Cueva* 6(1950).129-130.
EVANS, E. M.: *Bulletin of the School of Oriental and African Studies* 13(1950).531-534.
O'CONNOR, J. D.: *Le Meître Phonetique* 3(1950).34-36.
TRAGER, G. L.: *Language* 26(1950).152-158.
GONZALES, L.: *Palaestra Latina* 22(1951).139.
ZGUSTA, L.: *Lingua Posnaniensis* 5(1955).231-234.

4.5 **Tone Languages** (1948).
BLACK, J. W.: *Quarterly Journal of Speech* 34(1948).519-520.
WONDERLY, W. L.: *International Journal of American Linguistics* 14(1948).60.
HERZOG W.: *International Journal of American Linguistics* 48(1949).
236-244.
TRAGER, G. L.: *Journal of English and German Philology* 48(1949).
238-286.
FLOREZ, L.: *Boletin del Instituto Caro y Cueva* 6(1950).127-128.
LI, F-K.: *Language* 26(1950).401-403.

4.6 **Axioms and Procedures for Reconstruction** (1950).
TRAGER, G. L.: *Studies in Linguistics* 9(1951).20.

4.7 **Language in Relation to a Unified Theory of the Structure of Human Behavior** (1st. ed., 1954, 1955, 1960; 2nd ed., 1967).

HOIJER, H.: *Language* 31(1955).485-488.

DAELMAN, J.: *La Revue de Questions Scientifique* 5:16(1955).627-628.

SHELDON, C.: *General Semantics Bulletin* 18-19(1955-56).99-103.

GAUTIER, M.: *Journal de Psychologie Normale et Pathologique* 55:2 (1956).205-206.

NEWMAN, S.: *International Journal of American Linguistics* 22(1956). 84-88.

CHIOCI: *Revista de Filosofia* (Torino), 2(1956).223-224.

D. S.: *Chronique Sociale* 1(1958).661.

NEWMAN, S.: *International Journal of American Linguistics* 27 (1961).63-64.

FIELDING, H.: *The Year's Work in English Studies* 36(1956).37.

HOIJER, H.: *Language* 32(1956).477-479.

ROBINS, R. H.: *Le Maître Phonetique* 3:106(1956).38-40.

MILLER, G.: *Contemporary Psychology* 1(1956).19-20.

CARROLL, J.: *Psychological Abstracts* 2918(1957).

MCQUOWN, N.: *American Anthropologist* 59(1957).189-192.

RUYTINX, J.: *Revue Internationale de Philosophie* (Brussels), 40:2 (1957).232-235.

SIVERTSEN, E.: *Norsk Tideskrift for Sprogvidenskap* 18(1958)398-413.

ZGUSTA, L.: *Archiv Orientálni* (Prague), 26(1958).285-287.

GAUTHIER, M.: *Word* 16(1960).392-398.

ANON.: *English Language Teaching* 23(1969).189-190.

BZEDA, A.: *Lingua Posnaniensis* 14(1969).140-146.

HYMES, D.: *American Anthropologist* 71(1969).361-363.

SMITH, N. J.: *Philosophy and Rhetoric* 2(1969).118-119.

4.8 **Kenneth L. Pike: Selected Writings** (1972).

MCQUOWN, N.: *American Anthropologist* 76(1974).931-932.

HOUSEHOLDER, FRED W.: *Journal of Linguistics* 11(1975).104-117.

4.9 **Grammatical Analysis** (1977).

BREND, R. M.: *Lingua* 45(1978).91-94.

4.10 **Tagmemics, Discourse and Verbal Art** (1981).

KOKTOVA, E.: *Journal of Pragmatics* 7(1983).240-242.

BREND, R. M.: *Word* 34(1983).133-134.

4.11 **Linguistic Concepts** (1982).

KOKTOVA, E.: *Journal of Pragmatics* 9(1985).155-161.

4.12 **Text and Tagmeme** (1983).

KOKTOVA, E.: *Journal of Pragmatics* 9(1985).155-161.

5. RECOGNITIONS, AWARDS

1952-53 Rockefeller Foundation Grant

1960   Alumnus of the Year, Gordon College

1961   President, Linguistic Society of America

1966   Distinguished Faculty Achievement Award, University of Michigan

1967   Doctor of Humanities, Huntington College

1973   Doctor of Humane Letters, University of Chicago

1974   Presidential Merit Member, The Philippines

1974-79 Charles C. Fries Chair of Linguistics, University of Michigan

1978   President, Linguistic Association of Canada and the United States

1978   Docteur Honoris Causa, University of Sorbonne (René Descartes Université)

1984   Nominated for the Nobel Peace Prize

1985   Elected to the National Academy of Sciences

1987   Nominated for Nobel Peace Prize

6. BOOK PUBLICATIONS ON K. L. PIKE

EUNICE V. PIKE: *Ken Pike: Scholar and Christian*. Dallas, Tx.: Summer Institute of Linguistics, 1981, 268 pp.

Languages for Peace: Tribute to Kenneth L. Pike. Lake Bluff, Illinois: Jupiter Press, 1985, 33 pp.

[Grateful acknowledgment is made to Dr. Alan C. Wares—bibliographer of the Summer Institute of Linguistics—and to Eunice V. Pike for aid in compiling the bibliography.]

APPENDICES

1. Biography of Kenneth Lee Pike

By Ruth M. Brend

Kenneth Lee Pike was born June 9, 1912 in Woodstock, Conn., U.S.A. His parents, who had served as missionaries in Alaska, had a profound influence on him in his early years and it seems natural that, while a student at Gordon College, he applied for missionary service in China. However, to his great disappointment, he was turned down—because of "nervousness" and, perhaps, for his poor phonetic performance as his sister, Eunice, suggests. (I am indebted to Eunice V. Pike for allowing me to draw extensively on her publication *Ken Pike: Scholar and Christian,* Dallas: Summer Institute of Linguistics, 1981, for much of the biographical information here.)

Shortly after, in 1935, Pike and four others comprised the entire student body of the second summer session of a small linguistics training course, held in a farmhouse in Sulphur Springs, Arkansas. The head of the school, W. Cameron Townsend, subsequently became the founder and General Director of the Summer Institute of Linguistics (SIL) and its sister organization, the Wycliffe Bible Translators (WBT). Townsend then had (and SIL-WBT still have) the main goal of training students in linguistics in order to prepare them for learning, analyzing and reducing to writing the unwritten languages of the world, and providing for those languages a literature, including the New Testament.

After spending the summer with grammar studies, ethnology, and phonetics, Pike accompanied Mr. Townsend (as well as Mrs. Townsend, the Townsends' niece, and the other students) to Mexico. There Pike began to study the language of the Mixtecos in a remote village in the state of Oaxaca. He was delighted to be in a foreign country, endeavoring to serve God. Many of the details of those often-difficult early years may be found in *Two Thousand Tongues to Go,* by Ethel Wallace and Mary Bennett, New York: Harper and Bros., 1959 and in the volume by Eunice V. Pike (cited above). From the beginning Pike showed great aptitude at learning and analyzing the language, and he became greatly interested in Sapir's *Language,* which he had discovered in a Mexico City library.

The following summer (1936) Pike returned to the little Arkansas Institute and taught phonetics to 16 students, one of whom was Eugene A. Nida. Nida, having already had previous linguistic training, was able to advise Pike on the Mixteco grammatical materials, and to introduce him to Bloomfield's *Language.*

For the next several years, with the exception of the summers, Pike continued to study in the Mixteco area, and to help his sister (and partner), Eunice, in the analysis of the Mazateco language. He also began to prepare a manuscript on how sounds are made, designed for beginning field workers.

In the summer of 1937, Townsend suggested that Pike attend the Linguistic Institute of the Linguistic Society of America at the University of Michigan—where Edward Sapir was to be on the faculty, and Charles C. Fries was to be the Director. Before the Institute began, Pike sent Sapir a copy of his phonetics manuscript, and, during the summer, Sapir showed it to Bernard Bloch and Morris Swadesh. All urged him to continue. It was this summer, because of his short informal sessions with both faculty and students, helping them to produce glottalized stops, that Sapir began referring to him as "glottal stop Pike."

In the summer of 1938, Pike left the LSA Institute early, in order to co-direct the SIL school with Nida. One of the students there, who was planning to joint the Institute's work abroad, was a previous acquaintance— Mr. Townsend's niece, who had accompanied the group to Mexico three years before. By summer's end, Pike and Evelyn Griset became engaged and were married in Mexico City three months later. They have had three children, Judith (who, with her husband, is a member of the Mexico branch of SIL), Barbara (a librarian, whose husband works with a computing firm in Michigan, and who has two children) and Stephen (a musician, married to the former Patricia McKaughan, a psychologist whose father is a member of the linguistics faculty of the University of Hawaii).

By the fall of the 1938, Pike had presented a couple of scholarly papers and produced a 2-page "Phonemics Work Sheet"—forerunners of his *Phonemics* and *Tone Languages*. In the latter he formalized the procedures he had used himself in the analysis of Mixteco and in his consultation in the analysis of Mazateco.

At the LSA Institute Pike studied with, or heard lectures by, Sapir, Bloomfield, Bloch, Swadesh, Harris, Trager, Sturtevant, M. Cowan, Hockett, and Voegelin (among others). Fries arranged for his summer credits to be applied towards a Ph.D. which he received in August, 1941; his dissertation was later published under the title *Phonetics: a Technic for the Description of Sounds*.

After his marriage, Pike spent the winters among the Mixtecos with his wife and growing family, and the summers divided between the LSA Institute in Ann Arbor and the SIL school which moved to the campus of the University of Oklahoma in 1941. Pike and Nida co-directed the SIL Institute for more than a decade—that is, until Nida began to work full time with the American Bible Society. At that time Pike became the sole director of the Oklahoma SIL Institute.

In the Spring of 1942, at the invitation of Fries, Pike prepared materials on the intonation of American English for students at the University of Michigan's English Language Institute. These materials were later incorporated in Pike's *Pronunciation:* Vol. I of *An Intensive Course in English for Latin*

American Students and in *The Intonation of American English.* He has often acknowledged his immense debt to Professor Fries for support and encouragement over many years.

In 1943, Pike travelled to Peru where, after interviews with government and university officials, he received an invitation for SIL to begin study of the indigenous languages of that country. A decade later, he helped in beginning similar contacts with the government of Brazil.

During the late forties and early fifties, a "typical" year involved doing research and teaching in the Winter Semester at the University of Michigan, teaching and directing the Oklahoma SIL in the summer, and working on the Mixteco language analysis and preparing publications in Mixteco in Mexico during the fall. (Donald and Ruth Stark also began to help with the Mixteco work during this period.)

Pike had become the first President of SIL at its incorporation in 1942 — a position which he held until 1979. He was director of two sessions of the Institute's Jungle Camp in southern Mexico in 1947 and 1948. As SIL President, he travelled to Australia and England to help initiate summer sessions of the Institute there and, eventually, presided over a total of eight schools in countries as diverse as West Germany and Japan. He also personally directed the University of Oklahoma Institute through 1971, and he continues to be on its faculty each summer.

Appointed as Associate Professor at the University of Michigan in 1948, Pike obtained a unique arrangement. At first he spent one semester per year at the university, and the rest of the year with SIL. Later, this was changed to one academic year in residence and one away, and still later to a three year cycle of two years in residence, with one year away. He was appointed Professor in 1955, received the Distinguished Faculty Achievement Award in 1966, and was named to the Charles C. Fries Chair of Linguistics in 1974. Before retiring from the University in 1979, he served as Chair of the Department of Linguistics and, simultaneously, as Director of its English Language Institute.

Probably the non-academic campus activity he enjoyed most was the tri-weekly noon swim with the Flounders (a group of faculty and community men who play a frenzied game of water polo, and then have lunch together, accompanied by a host of "traditions"). Another non-academic activity over the years was the teaching of a student Bible Class on Sunday mornings when in Ann Arbor. The Pikes frequently opened their home to his university students, as well as to those in the Bible classes and in other campus religious groups.

The Mixteco New Testament was finished in 1957. After that, Pike spent his off-campus time directing field workshops for his SIL colleagues, assisting them with their analyses of the indigenous languages of Latin America, Africa, Nepal, Papua New Guinea, the Philippines, India, and Indonesia.

The departure of Nida from SIL caused Pike to feel the necessity of branching out into publishing on grammatical analysis. (Previously he had published solely on phonology, although he had obtained considerable field experience in all aspects of language in his own work and in his consultation with other SIL colleagues.) In the late 1940's the germ of a linguistic theory, encompassing many facets of language, emerged. A major work on that theory (later named "tagmemics") appeared first in preliminary form in 1954, 1955, and 1960, with a second revised edition appearing in 1967, under the title *Language in Relation to a Unified Theory of the Structure of Human Behavior.* The frequent oscillation between teaching and research on the campus with field investigations and consultation throughout the world resulted in an analytical theory which is especially useful in the analysis of unwritten languages. Numerous tagmemic publications have followed. Other than Pike himself, probably the major contributors have been Robert Longacre in grammar and Eunice Pike in phonology, although many other scholars have contributed to it and utilized it in various degrees. Anthropologists today often use the terms "etic" and "emic", without knowing that they were invented by Pike. Not only linguistic and anthropological scholars, but also psychologists, sociologists, musicologists, among others, have found the theory to be useful in their own disciplines. Listings of many tagmemic publications can be found in RUTH M. BREND, "Tagmemic Theory: An Annotated Bibliography, and Appendix I," *Journal of English Linguistics* 4(1970).7-45 and 6(1972).1-16, as well as in the bibliographies included in chapters in RUTH M. BREND and KENNETH L. PIKE, eds., *Tagmemics: Vol. I, Aspects of the Field, Vol. II, Theoretical Discussion,* The Hague: Mouton 1976.

Since retiring from the University in 1979, Pike has not slowed down. A check of his publications since that date shows that his recent production is nearly as prolific as previously. In addition, Pike (usually accompanied by his wife) continues to direct workshops abroad and to teach (including a recent short course in Beijing). When in the U.S. the Pikes live near a SIL center in Dallas, Texas, where they both assist the Institute in various ways, and Pike serves as an Adjunct Professor at the University of Texas in Arlington.

Perhaps, for many, their most vivid memory of Pike is his performance of a monolingual demonstration. In front of an audience (usually composed of linguists and non-linguists) he meets for the first time, a native speaker of a language, the identity of which is also unknown to Pike. Using only a few props such as sticks, flowers, leaves and stones, but with *no* verbal translation, Pike demonstrates how much of the language he can analyze in less than 90 minutes or so. Even to those who have seen the demonstration a number of times, it still appears a "tour de force" of courage and ability. An abbreviated taped version of one demonstration can be seen via film (reference above in the bibliography, p. 31).

Pike himself would clearly prefer to be known for his contribution to the Kingdom of God. His continued efforts today, on the eve of his 75th birthday, in teaching, writing, advising and encouraging, are directed towards that end. (Many of his chapel talks, given at the SIL summer sessions, have been published and are included in the religious section of his bibliography).

The citation given when he was honored by the University of Chicago, describing him as the epitome of a Christian scholar and gentleman, describes a goal toward which he continues to strive.

2. Kenneth Lee Pike as Teacher

By ALTON LEWIS BECKER
(Ann Arbor, Michigan)

I was Pike's student at Michigan from 1961 to 1966. There had been many before me and would be many after, but I hope I can speak for all of them in this attempt to describe the way he taught us.

Going in for linguistics with Pike was quite comparable to going out for a sport. I think he saw his students as almost all capable of great academic achievement if they were willing to work hard and develop their abilities. The first course I took from him was Phonemics. Ruth Brend was his assistant, then an upper-level graduate student along with many others who would be first class linguists: Charles Fillmore, William Wong, John Gumperz, Ilse Lehiste, Sanford Shane, Andrew Koutsoudas, Velma Pickett, and many others. It was a fine place to be a student in the Sixties.

Ruth Brend taught us articulatory phonetics and Pike lectured on phonemics. It was in that mode that many of us were first taught by him, getting the absolutely necessary phonetic skills from Brend and from Pike a kind of spellbinding performance, often our first real taste of linguistics. The key issue in this first course was the nature of the linguistic unit. What is it we study when we do linguistics? The answer was clear: a transcription of speaking. He insisted on what was then called, "hugging the phonetic ground." We had to learn to transcribe actual discourse phonetically, and we were drilled over and over again on this. One of the first assignments was to eavesdrop on an actual conversation and transcribe it, just a few lines. This was data, etic data, already, of course, interpreted by an observer. Pike was insistent on this, too: that there was always a knower in the known, that even phonetic representations were non-unique.

This was made clear to us in what came to be known as "monolingual" demonstrations, meaning that Pike and his informant did not use a common language. Pike spoke Mixtec and the informant, often a foreign student from the class, spoke Thai or Swahili or whatever. This remains a remarkable pedagogical device. It helps us become self-conscious of our English bias and move closer to the utopian goal of an emic perspective on a distant language. Pike's students were taught to shudder at the thought of asking an informant, in English, "How do you say, 'The book is on the table' in your language?"

We all knew that one day it would be our turn to go to the blackboard and transcribe from an unknown language while Pike watched and commented. He was a sharp critic, but always fair. If he disagreed he would argue strongly,

but, every now and then admit defeat. If any student ever laughed at some-
one else's transcription, Pike would get quite angry. We learned from making
errors.

The lectures were often quite personal, about a problem in phonemic
analysis he had confronted helping a missionary in Brazil, or about an
argument he had just had with Charles Hockett at the Linguistics Society
meeting. Linguistics was very much people and experience.

At the same time his theory of language, Tagmemics, was taking shape
for us: slots and fillers, hierarchy, multiple constraints—all shaped from real,
particular data, most of which was gathered in the classroom. There was
homework every day and it was graded severely, always half of it by Pike.

After this first course in phonemics we took smaller courses with Pike,
in American Indian Languages, Discourse Analysis, Advanced Phonemics,
and then seminars. All of those courses would engage a major theoretical
concern of Pike's. At that time what we might now call paradigmatics was a
"frontier"—the point where what we thought we knew about language touched
the unknown. He prodded us to get to the frontier. We had a great sense of
academic excitement as we explored the matrix as a device to handle complexity
and the four (or six or twelve)-celled tagmeme, using discourse data often
fresh from the field, Choctaw, Navaho, Fore, Nepali.

A required course for doctoral students was Pike's seminar in Descriptive
Linguistics. It was built around a bibliography Pike had published called "Live
Issues in Descriptive Linguistics." We were required to do a couple dozen
skim reports—one page essays on our readings, assigned or self-selected.
And twice in the seminar we had to conduct the seminar, first on a topic
from the bibliography, then on a topic of our own choice. On these two topics
we were expected to know *everything* that had been said and to handle seminar
questions on them. I remember I did Pronouns first and then Discourse
Analysis. The rival school of discourse analysis at that time was headed by
Zellig Harris, for whom Pike had great respect but with whose work he
often argued. I think he felt that formalism of the sort that Harris sought,
first in morphology and syntax, then in discourse study, was elegant but
essentially oversimplified the data. There was more smear and indeterminacy
in language than formal structuralism seemed to admit, and also more openness
to the larger context. It was in these terms that we discussed formalism of
linguistics, "current in what it affirms," he often said, "but wrong in what it
denies."

Pike's other seminars were always experimental. I was one of many in
those seminars who were asked to co-author papers with Pike. Here we were
taught intensively. I was to work on the prefixes to the Navaho verb. It was
a very tough descriptive problem. What we attempted was reconstruction of
an historical paradigm which could sort out the fusions and irregularities of
the present system. Pike was anxious to show that his new tool, matrix analysis,
could handle tough descriptive problems with some elegance. He chose Navaho
because it was an interest of Harry Hoijer, and the article was for an issue

of IJAL dedicated to Hoijer. I rewrote the paper more than a dozen times as Pike opened up things I hadn't seen or showed me problems in my analysis. There is nothing more important in academic training than this kind of apprenticeship.

I have often been asked if Pike's Protestant Christianity got in the way in his classes. I think not. I think it strengthened his arguments, and I write from the perspective of a non-theist. Pike's strong theism was, for us, the ground on which he built his insistence that people who spoke languages with few speakers must be helped to come into the present with their languages alive. And it is the foundation on which his sense of the "emic" was built. Pike's theism seemed to make radical relativism possible, even necessary, when dealing with the close connection of language and worldview or consciousness. He could be a cultural relativist, and allow multiple emic perspectives on the world, because he was a theist. And besides that, of course, he had access to all the unexpected things S.I.L. linguists were finding as they studied languages all over the world. If any of us had the temerity to suggest a facile universal, Pike would find four exceptions from Central American languages alone. His memory seemed unlimited.

The final stage of Pike's teaching was for many of us his chairing of our doctoral dissertations. That meant Saturday mornings in his attic study at home, after a thorough whipping at pingpong. (He was a very aggressive athlete, and most of his students learned this one way or another; he once invited me to go play water polo and I did and almost died in a maelstrom of professors' bodies. Play was wild. I could not push a professor's face underwater with the palm of my hand, so I quit. I asked Pike why he did it and he said it was to expend his aggressions: "Otherwise I would take it out on students like you.")

As a doctoral chair he was very good. It was clear from the start that the dissertation was your own work. He would help when asked. Most of us chose problems he was interested in. Mine was to develop the four-celled Tagmeme as a tool for describing the subject of English clauses (as a place, a function, and a choice in one or more paradigms). It was just before Charles Fillmore's exciting work on case grammar, and Pike shared with me the discussions he had had with Fillmore. it was always encouraging when one disagreed with Pike, to be told to follow one's own ideas, to share in the fun of building a theory. He took me to the Georgetown Roundtable with him in 1965, where I gave my first paper. He coached me thoroughly, particularly on the question period. He told me you could win the paper and still lose the match in the question period, so he got me ready.

This has all been in the past tense to convey its particularity. I am talking of Pike as a teacher, and that ended for me in 1966, when I completed my dissertation. After that we became colleagues. Pike is still teaching, but those years at Michigan are over.

I think many of us are still challenged by the frontiers he guided us to, fired by the motives he sparked. For me the challenge has been the linguistics of particularity, but there are many different stories to tell here, too. The point is, I guess, that lighting those fires in our minds is what makes him not just a very good teacher but a great one.

3. Kenneth L. Pike as Friend and Colleague within the Summer Institute of Linguistics

By ROBERT E. LONGACRE
(Arlington, Texas)

I first met Kenneth L. Pike the summer of 1945 when, as a very insecure person, but one definitely interested in linguistics and Bible translation, I went to the Norman SIL (= Summer Institute of Linguistics). The first time I saw him in class, like many people, I was scared and terrified that he would call on me to recite or say something in that first phonemics class. I soon got acquainted with him however, and had occasion to see him in private the first week I was there. I found a warm-hearted human being. This was the beginning of a friendship of many years.

That was the summer in which Pike had his book *Tone Languages* in mimeograph form for student use. It was in press but would be awhile yet coming out. To me fell the job of duplicating a part of the book, i.e., turning the crank of the mimeograph. I recall one night when I was working late at the job and nobody else was around. Suddenly the door burst open, Pike strode in on his long legs, holding a bag in his hand, took a big roll of some kind out of the bag, stuck it in my mouth, turned around, and walked out without saying a word.

At the end of the summer, Ken hired me to strap his trunks and suitcases and finish some of his packing in preparation for going down to Mexico. He and (wife) Evie were on their way there.

The book *Tone Languages* that I had helped mimeograph was published. When my wife and I finally went to Mexico in the fall of 1946 and were assigned to the Trique Indians of Oaxaca, *Tone Languages* became a sort of linguistic Bible for me. We had a very difficult tone system to analyze and I went by the book. Meanwhile, with encouragement from Ken and others, I was able to keep at it. I finally decided that the only way to make any sense out of the whole analytical mess in Trique was to posit, contrary to the book, that there were five phonemic pitch levels in Trique and combinations of those five levels. The book said that tone levels could be found up to four but probably no more.

Finally, Ken and I got together at a workshop in Mitla in southern Mexico. I had a twelve-year-old boy as a language helper. His voice was still unchanged and high-pitched, and he spread the tones apart in a way which gave us maximum ease in hearing. I had the material lined up in frames the way Ken told us to do in the Tone Language book, and in about ten minutes we had given a very clear demonstration that there were five phonemic pitch levels in Trique. Ken leaned back in his chair and drawled, "Well, I never expected to hear anything like that." But although we were able to show on very short order that there were five such levels, the working out of many of the details, many of the phonemic glides between levels which I had found very hard to hear, continued to prove difficult. For the balance of the workshop Ken assisted me on getting some of those tone combinations pinned down and understanding better the workings of the *system* in which the tones appear.

Eventually, I had the draft of a paper on the five phonemic tone levels in Trique. Ken was my consultant and we squeezed out hours of work at the ends of busy days at Branch and Corporation Conference. My paper was prolix. It had many loose bolts and screws. It was too big. I tried to cover not only the phonology of the five tones, but also their use within the grammar of the language. Ken encouraged me to cut it in half, and do a good job on the first part. But there were some tense moments. As I have said, my paper was badly in need of attention and I was somewhat proud of my work and had not learned as I have learned in years since then to value criticism. At one point, late at night when we were both tired, Ken looked me in the eye and said, "Your paper has so many non-sequiturs that you need to take a course in symbolic logic somewhere." It took me a couple of years to quite forgive Ken for that remark. I repeat, however, it was late at night and the paper would have tried the patience of almost any linguistic consultant at that stage. The point is, however, that the paper got done, Ken helped me find a publisher, and this, my "maiden paper", finally appeared in print.

I recall that one time early in our residence among the Triques, Gwen and I went down to Tlaxiaco to meet Ken, his wife Evie, and their two children who were on their way out of Mixteco country. I will always remember seeing Ken coming down the road with daughter Barbara on his shoulders and how glad we were to see them, to "talk shop" with them, and to get further acquainted as human beings.

From 1949 on, I began to teach during the summers at Norman, Oklahoma. One thing I soon came to value was the further informal education I received from Ken on a continuing basis. Ken had graciously extended to me an "open door policy". I could drop in almost any time on this fantastically busy man and talk with him for awhile regarding linguistics, field work, and my own involvement in it all. I always got a very cordial reception from him. His fanatical insistence on professional competence was built into my fiber at that period. He insisted that we read papers at conferences and publish. He insisted that the published papers be of good professional quality. Then, too, from the Norman years, we recall Ken as a volleyball player, a very skillful spiker of the ball; it wasn't always too comfortable to be on the other side when he spiked the ball down your neck. Those years are also unforgettable in terms of Ken's chapel talks, talks which now have given birth to a series of books which have had a broad spectrum of usefulness to the Christian public.

I also recall Ken from SIL Mexico Branch and Corporation Conferences. I recall Ken as debater and as chairman of long and difficult sessions. Ken set the ideal that "open dissent is better than feigned agreement". He felt that God leads a group of people who want to serve Him through open and honest debate, through disagreement, through voting, and then closing ranks after the vote. We could argue vigorously together on the conference floor and go out and have coffee together at the first break. We learned that it is better to risk even an occasional show of bad temper in public than to "short-circuit" the democratic process. Ken as chairman was incomparable. I especially remember his careful respect for minority points of view and his refusal to allow anybody to run roughshod over them in a deliberative assembly.

Then I recall Ken as the originator of what has since been called "tagmemics". I was there at the birth, I suppose, of it all. I got to Norman two weeks early the summer of 1949 because we had been at Lake Francis previously. Here I was able to hear the original series of lectures from Ken on the search for a ruler of Grammar which he then called "the Grammeme." I sat open-mouthed through it all. You see, in those days, no one had tried to do much with syntax. Syntax was considered to be the stepchild of descriptive linguistics. Grammar consisted of phonemic statements and a description of verb and noun morphology with maybe two or three pages of syntax. In a year or two after tagmemics got started, many people in SIL and the Mexican Branch began to do Syntax, and did it with a measure of confidence. That we were all subsequently swamped in the Chomskian Revolution has somewhat obscured this development, but for those of us who passed through it, the Tagmemic Revolution which made syntax possible for us, was a truly exciting development.

Though I still hold to the basic assumptions of tagmemics and probably always will, as time passed, I came to differ somewhat with Pike. At first our courses were parallel, then we began to diverge on particulars—although we have continued, all through the years, to agree on certain basic principles in our approach to language. For example, I wanted to implement the notion of hierarchy so as to set up tagmemes on various levels instead of just at the level of the simple sentence. The summer of 1954, Ken and I were more or less in head-on collision all summer. Ken had just published Vol. I of what became his large work *Language in Relation to a Unified Theory of the Structure of Human Behavior* (=LRUTSHB), and I was dissatisfied with what I read—for the reason already stated. Finally, I was given the privilege one Thursday night, to present to a linguistic seminar why I differed with Pike and why I was unhappy with what he was doing at that time. I found it painful to disagree with him, and I prepared very carefully my piece like a lawyer preparing for a case in court. So, I got up and said my piece, sat down and wondered what would happen. A few comments were made and finally Ken Pike got up and said, "During the last few weeks I very scrupulously concealed the fact that I am now in substantial agreement with Dr. Longacre." This was certainly a surprise and totally unanticipated by myself and others. Ken was simply playing at this point the role of a good coach and felt that if he would not tell me that he fundamentally agreed with me, I would sharpen my arguments much more and would present a much better case. That, of course, is exactly what happened. The differences between us were soon cleared up. My influence on Pike's thinking at this time can be seen in the differences between the wording of the second volume of LRUTSHB as compared with that of the first volume.

Pike had begun to hold international workshops which proved to be a considerable success in helping people to solve linguistic problems and write publishable linguistic papers. Eventually it was suggested to me that maybe I should hold a workshop or two also. The first one was to be in the Philippines in 1967-68. I wanted to go and I wrote up a proposal for the National Science Foundation. On its being rejected, Pike suggested that we could apply to the Office of Education in Washington where he had some contacts. But to make the venture feasible it was necessary to put Pike in the role of principal investigator and myself in the role of supporting investigator—although I was to do all the "on the spot" work. We sent in our proposal and waited. The grant was approved just before Gwen and I were to leave.

I recall when Pike came to visit us at the Nasuli center in the Philippines (as Principal Investigator it was quite necessary that he come), however, I did something that I never had done before: I sat him down and said, "Now it's your turn to listen to me" and speedily wore the man out with what I thought we had found out at the workshop.

Through the years Pike has shown admirable toleration and the ability to encourage people to work even along lines that he found personally distasteful. He has encouraged independence on the part of the various SIL's—independence on the part of people who teach at them. Pike did not want to be surrounded by a bunch of "yes men"; much less by a bunch of clones.

In the early 50's, Pike encouraged me to go on for a Ph.D. At first I was dismayed—I wanted to get back to the Triques, continuing to go on preparing for translation among them. But, Pike urged me to do it, and I was accepted at the University of Pennsylvania. I was the fifth one to acquire a doctorate within SIL. At one time we lived in Pike's house in Ann Arbor. I taught courses in his place at University of Michigan and I taught his Sunday School class. I soon came to appreciate Pike's capacities as a teacher.

It was interesting to live in Ken's house. I recall that one of our next door neighbors said that she always was impressed because she often heard Pike and Evie and the children singing around in the house as they went about their various tasks. We learned in many ways that the Pikes had a very light hold on the things of this world and their value system included a lot of things of a non-material and more important sort.

And so we have valued Ken and Evie's friendship down through the years. It still is one of the most restful and significant experiences that Gwen and I can have—to be invited down to Pike's for a quiet meal with a discussion afterwards. Pike used to say that Charles Carpenter Fries had been to him a "giant shade tree in which he had grown in his young professional years."

I can say the same thing about Kenneth L. Pike. He has been *my* shade tree during the years of my early linguistic growth. I owe a lot to him—probably much more than even I, myself, realize for the encouragement and help he has given to me in the years I've worked with him in SIL.

4. Kenneth L. Pike: Mentor and Friend

By PETER H. FRIES
(Tucson, Arizona)

Perhaps I should begin this piece with a disavowal, because, while I feel that Kenneth L. Pike has been a great influence on my life, I have never been formally in one of his classes. It turns out that in this respect, my relation with him recapitulates his relation with my father. In each case, the influence of the older person on the younger has been great, but in each case it has occurred through informal channels. When I was a child, my father, Charles Fries, took an interest in Kenneth and therefore as I grew up, the Pikes were a permanent part of my life, both academic and personal. Some of my earliest memories as a child were of what seemed to me endless conversations about linguistics at the dinner table between Kenneth and my father. When I was an undergraduate at the University of Michigan, at my father's suggestion, I began my formal training in linguistics at the summer course of the Summer Institute of Linguistics in Norman, Oklahoma (where Pike was the Director). My father's argument was that the course of study at the Norman SIL provided the best practical introduction to field linguistics available at the time. He was right. We spent the morning hours working on phonetics, phonemics and grammar, our afternoons were devoted to training in anthropology, literacy, translation and other topics. Kenneth was not one of the regular first year faculty at that time, but his presence was definitely felt even by the first year students. For example, it was clearly through his influence that even in 1958, we students were taught that we must deal with discourse as an integral part of linguistics. Occasionally he would lecture to us on grammar in the morning, but for me, the most memorable of his contributions occurred when he presented his materials on English intonation. For some reason, this material was relegated to the afternoon. The entire first year class met as a group in a large unairconditioned auditorium beginning at about 2:00, during what seemed the absolute hottest part of that hot Oklahoma summer. (This was my first experience with temperatures that stayed over 100 degrees for more than a few days at a time, and so experiencing a summer in the south in unairconditioned buildings was a real change for a boy who had grown up in Michigan. In contrast to my reaction, Kenneth seemed to thrive in the heat.) We were perhaps about two hundred in that room. And after Kenneth explained some of the essentials of English intonation, and illustrated how it was transcribed and was to be read, he had us read some material that he had transcribed. Most of the material we read consisted of poems by Robert Frost which Kenneth had translated from a record of Robert Frost reading his own poetry. We were each asked to read a short portion in turn and Pike would tell us whether we had read it correctly or not. If we had not, then the next person would get a try—and the next and the next and the next..., if it proved a difficult passage. As was to be expected, many of us made mistakes. Some of our mistakes arose because we were unfamiliar with the notational system, some arose because some of the passages were difficult to render even when one knew what was desired. I remember that one passage in particular was very difficult, because it required a down-step in pitch while moving to an accented syllable. We all accented the syllable with the higher pitch. As I remember it, a whole row of students, including me, missed that passage before Kenneth finally decided to demonstrate what was happening for us. All in all, it was a very memorable experience for me (and I still can recite most of the poem with the proper intonation, I think).

One feature that characterizes Kenneth is that he believes in challenging those around him. For example, while I was taking the first year course at Norman, he suggested that I attend the colloquium that was held every Monday evening for advanced students and staff. Many aspects of the presentations were beyond me, and I would not have attended them had he not made his suggestion, but I am happy that he encouraged me to come. I suppose that in fact my experience in these presentations mirrors Kenneth's theory about delivering lectures. As I recall, he used to say that one should divide the lecture into three portions of about equal sizes. The first third should be material that everyone can understand, the second third should be beyond the beginners and should challenge most of the audience, while the last portion should present information that is new to everyone and challenges even the most advanced listener.

Kenneth has been concerned to bring novices efficiently into the mainstream of the discipline and to help them to quickly become contributing members of the group. One aspect of this concern has been his continuing interest in providing materials for beginning students. This theme runs through all his publications, from the publication of *Phonemics* to his recent publications *Grammatical Analysis* and *Linguistic Concepts*. Of course his concern for the beginner also includes careful thought about the content necessary for a program of study for beginning field workers, and one finds tucked away in his bibliography a description of the program at the Norman SIL together with some of the motivations for the shape that that program took. In addition to care for beginning students, Kenneth has also been concerned for the more advanced students and the beginning teachers. One result of this concern of course includes giving younger scholars opportunities to present their material to friendly audiences. Indeed my first general lectures were delivered at the Monday night forum of SIL Norman. But in addition to this fairly obvious step, he was instrumental in organizing support for beginning teachers. I experienced this when I returned to Norman in the early 1960's to get a more extensive grounding in field linguistics by studying and teaching in the program. Because each course was being taught by a large number of teaching assistants with varying past experience, each course had been placed in the charge of one advanced person, and that person had the responsibility of organizing the course, determining what would be taught, and then making sure that we teaching assistants understood the material, knew what the issues and probable questions were, and had a basic idea of how to present the materials. Each day, we budding teachers were given a lesson plan, and we went over it in detail with our department head. It was made clear to us that each day we had to cover at least a minimum of the material (and that minimum was described for us), because at the end of a couple of weeks we teaching assistants would change sections and deal with a new group of students. While there is no doubt that the whole experience was regimented, there is also no doubt that I was thereby enabled to teach a far better course than I could possibly have done with less help. In addition, since much of the discussion in the staff briefings concerned linguistic issues, I learned a great deal of linguistics from the experience. Finally, the experience gave me a background in teaching that was invaluable, since it gave me a content to teach, one suggestion of how to organize and teach it, and some experience with the issues that students saw and how the issues could be dealt with. In short, I feel that this experience was the best introduction to teaching linguistics that was available at the time.

Another feature that is typical of Kenneth is the fact that he consistently attempts to gain information from others. While Kenneth was not the only one to encourage me to read in various theories, he regularly encouraged me to look outside his theory to other theories and experiences. It was largely at his urging that I chose to do my graduate work at the University of Pennsylvania. I originally went to study with Zellig Harris, but also met Liskar, Hoenigswald and Hiz there, all of whom became very influential in my thinking. Similarly, at Norman, Pike strongly encouraged us to read Halliday's "Categories of the Theory of Grammar" when it first appeared in *Word*. It was through Kenneth that I first met Halliday and then Sidney Lamb, because he invited them to extended stays at Norman to discuss linguistics.

I would be remiss in my discussion of Kenneth if I omitted to mentioned his caring concern for others. When I received my Ph.D. degree, and moved to Wisconsin for my first job, Kenneth kept in touch in a way that was extremely helpful to me. In particular, as a recent Ph.D. I had a great deal of trouble figuring out what sorts of things I might write about. Kenneth took the time to discuss his ideas with me and to listen to mine, when I had something to say. His serving as a personal audience was an essential part of my development as a writer, for because of his serving as an audience, I was able to figure out what I had to say. In fact, most of my first articles began life as personal letters to him.

His interest in my career has continued, though it has changed as our relation has changed. I have become less dependent on a personal audience as the genesis of my writing, and our foci of interest have changed over the years. I am no longer explicitly working with the Tagmemic model (though I believe that almost everything I have done is compatible with that model); as a result our interactions have taken on the form of each keeping the other up to date on our recent thinking. One pleasurable exception to this pattern occurred when we collaborated on an article discussing the relation between Kenneth's work and that of Charles Fries. While it is obvious that Kenneth's interest in me has arisen for personal reasons, it is also obvious that his interest is not restricted to me. I know for a fact that he has played a similar role for a number of others; linguists and non-linguists alike. This has taken time and effort on his part. Sometimes the effort has required more energy than even he had. I well recall one occasion a number of years ago, when I was excitedly recounting some of my recent work to Kenneth and Evelyn, his wife, I discovered that he had fallen asleep. Evelyn and I continued talking until about a half an hour later, Kenneth chimed in with a relevant comment.

It is impossible to do justice to the way Kenneth has affected the people he has touched directly and indirectly. In this short essay, I have only tried to sketch a picture of the man by showing some of the ways he has touched my life.

5. Kenneth Pike and Diachronic Linguistics

By JOHN COSTELLO
(New York University)

It is ironic that the first procedural introduction to comparative linguistics, cast around a set of axioms and exercises, and entitled *Axioms and Procedures in Comparative Linguistics* (1951, revised 1957, see 1.7 in Bibliography) was written by a person who has claimed that he is not a "diachronic man": Kenneth L. Pike. It is also somewhat ironic that Pike has contributed in so many ways to diachronic linguistics via his work in synchronic theoretical linguistics.

Before he introduced the tagmeme (originally called *grameme*) as the linguistic unit of syntax, Pike had already theorized that all linguistic units possessed the property that they could be viewed in terms of their feature mode, their manifestation mode, and their distribution mode (U = F M D); thus, when the tagmeme later appeared in Pike's work, it predictably shared this property with the already-established phoneme and morpheme. Because of this, heretofore unknown parallels could be observed in synchronic linguistics at the levels of phonology, morphology, and syntax, not the least of which involve distinctions such as emic vs. etic, complementary distribution vs. free variation, and contrastive vs. characteristic environments.

Diachronic linguistics in general, and diachronic syntax in particular, on the other hand, have been far slower to realize the benefits of the high degree of generality which derives from Pike's definition of linguistic units.

Thus, for example, linguists working in some current non-tagmemic approaches
to the study of language change and linguistic reconstruction have observed
that in their models of language, there is a self-evident lack of parallelism
between syntactic and phonological reconstruction, because, by comparison
with phonology, there is, within their theoretical frameworks, no analogous
basis in syntax for the comparative method. Yet, just as the wave theory
enabled one to comprehend the occurrence of the Doppler Effect — originally
observed with sound energy — when one encountered alterations of radiation
in the form of visible light, and later in the rest of the electromagnetic
spectrum, so Pike's formula $U = F M D$ enables us to comprehend the
occurrence of the five basic patterns of replacement,[1] originally observed in
phonology, when encountered in morphology, and later, syntax. And it is
precisely because of the parallel occurrence of these patterns of replacement
at all levels of language that comparative reconstruction is possible at each
of these levels. It is particularly in the area of syntactic reconstruction, neglected
for so many decades in favor of phonological and morphological reconstruction,
and devoid of any methodology at all, tagmemic or otherwise, until fairly
recently, that the greatest benefits of Pike's theoretical contributions to
diachronic linguistics will be derived. For it is via tagmemics that we may
now apply the comparative method to reconstruct syntactic constructions,
their constituents, and the functions of these constituents.

Those who have followed closely developments in the various branches
of linguistics are aware of how far ahead of the field Pike has always been.
In synchronic linguistics, for example, investigators working in non-tagmemic
frameworks have only recently began to devote their attention to syntacto-
semantic role, government, and concord in the manner that Pike has been
doing since the development of the four-cell tagmeme. In diachronic linguistics,
Pike anticipated the possibility of reconstructing syntax via the tagmeme,
still in its infancy today, by the mid-fifties, years before other linguists
pondered this topic. So acute was his foresight that even then he perceived
that his theory predicted that in syntactic reconstruction, as in phonological
and morphological reconstruction, the retrieval of emic units would be possible,
whereas the retrieval of their etic manifestations might remain quite uncertain.
This is all the more impressive in light of the fact that even today, some
thirty years later, there are still many historical linguists who are surprised
once they observe this very same phenomenon for themselves.

To fail to mention the significance of Pike's faith in connection with his
linguistic work would be a gross oversight. Once while teaching at the Summer
Institute of Linguistics in Norman, Oklahoma, he observed to his students,
"Language reflects the image of God, so could you expect it to be anything
other than beautiful, elegantly patterned, glorious, and difficult?" For me, it
has been through Pike's contributions in linguistics that I have been able to
comprehend and appreciate these observations.

---

[1]One-to-one replacement, merger, split, obsolescence, and emergence.

6. The Influence of Kenneth Pike

By SYDNEY LAMB
(Rice University, Houston, Texas)

Much can be said about Kenneth Pike. Indeed, much has been said. Probably I can only repeat what has already been said many times, but at least it is in my own words enhanced by the credibility of a lifelong personal experience.

Ken Pike has touched many lives in many ways. As a teacher of linguistics, both in the classroom and in his ongoing series of workshops around the world, as well as through other teachers who have learned from him, he has taught thousands of people how to analyze and describe languages, and they have gone out and analyzed hundreds of languages spread over the entire range of the world's geography and of its typological and genetic groups. Under his guiding influence the linguists of the Summer Institute of Linguistics have probably done more actual descriptive lingusitic work during the past few decades than people of all other institutions combined.

In addition, Pike and his co-workers have brought literacy to thousands, eventually millions, of people in far-flung corners of the world, thus putting them and their posterity into more effective communication with the rest of mankind.

As a theoretical innovator in linguistics he has often been years ahead of others in discovering new ways of looking at linguistic phenomena. Some theoreticians find his theoretical work to be insufficiently formalized; they are thus misunderstanding its position among the current theories, and its purpose. There are different degrees and kinds of formalization appropriate to different goals in the study of language. For highly complex phenomena, language included, too much formalism is achieved only at the expense of loss of applicability to real life. Pike's Tagmemics has repeatedly proved itself in its usefulness in guiding the thinking and practice of ordinary working linguists.

His work and achievements have exhibited great diversity, yet they are all variations on a theme, the brotherhood of mankind: Bringing literacy to the fourth world, teaching others to do the same, providing theoretical frames which people can use in their work, all of which is concerned with promoting more effective communication among all peoples. This theme is brought to a focus in his famous monolingual demonstration, in which within a few minutes he establishes communication with another person without the use of any language previously known to him. The intellectual interest of this demonstration, great as it is, is overshadowed by the emotional impact of watching the communication dramatically develop, little by little but rapidly, and of seeing not only a developing basis of communication, but also the interpersonal warmth that grows along with it. This is what for me expresses the essence of his theme of lifelong devotion to his brothers and sisters around the world.

7. Pike's Tagmemic Theory

By ADAM MAKKAI
(University of Illinois, Chicago)

This brand of descriptive linguistics is, simultaneously, a philosophy and a world-view. Its main interest is that phenomena come in individual shapes and forms somewhat like human fingerprints or leaves of the same tree, which are never *identical;* yet they share so many *Basic Similarities* that it would be wrong not to co-classify them. Accordingly, the plane of individual manifestations is the *-etic* level (borrowed from phon*etics*), contrasted with the *-emic* level (borrowed from phon*emics*). The main initiator of the theory was K. L. Pike, but several dozen major American and foreign scholars have also made lasting contributions to this area and mode of research. Tagmemics sees language as having three components: Field, Wave and Particle; likening linguistics to physics. (At the 1927 Copenhagen Congress of Physicists it was finally agreed by N. Bohr, Max Planck, etc. that light was *both* wave *and* particle, not just the one or the other.) Words in isolation are particles; yet also in a field (i.e., related to each other); the word, when found in context, is in a discourse-field. Sounds overlap in speech, i.e., they come in waves; and so do semantic features which cannot always be ferreted out in a 1:1 fashion; furthermore, *time* goes on as people speak (wave view on a small scale). Tagmemics devotes its attention to Positive Data (as do Stratificational Grammar and other theories) since tagmemicists are basically field-linguists creating phonemically based alphabets for yet unwritten languages and grammars with libraries of texts ranging from the local fairy tale to modern UNESCO penicilin use instructions and nonsectarian translations of the Bible. In *tagmemics* one doesn't put an * in front of an utterance that does not occur, seeking explanations *why* the form failed to be recorded; only actual forms are shown. This gives *tagmemics* a heavily synchronic orientation although several tagmemicists have, independently, also worked on internal reconstruction and comparing different languages (e.g. J. Costello, S. Gudschinsky, R. E. Longacre). The chief value of tagmemics is its formidable battery of genuine data from exotic languages; under Pike's presidency of the SIL alone (1942-1979) 5,103 languages were catalogued as to their status in the *Ethnologue* (Barbara Grimes, Ed., 1978, Dallas, SIL). Literacy and Bilingual Education are chief concerns of tagmemicists on the practical level; theoretically, they have been moving more and more into cohesion, text-analysis and discourse (Evelyn G. Pike, Robert E. Longacre *et al.*).

TABULA GRATULATORIA

ARTHUR S. ABRAMSON
Storrs, Connecticut

JOHN ALGEO
Athens, Georgia

HORST ARNDT
Pulheim Stommeln, West Germany

ROBERT AUSTERLITZ
New York, New York

ROSE MARY BABITCH
Shippagan, New Brunswick, Canada

ULF BÄCKLUND
Umeà, Sweden

ALTON L. BECKER
Ann Arbor, Michigan

SIMON BELASCO
Columbia, South Carolina

DAVID & MARGARET
BENDOR-SAMUEL
Duncanville, Texas

JOHN & PAM BENDOR-SAMUEL
Dallas, Texas

MARSHALL D. BERGER
Orangeburg, N.Y.

KNUT BERGSLAND
Oslo, Norway

MACKIE JOSEPH VENET BLANTON
& LINDA LONON BLANTON
New Orleans, Louisiana

DWIGHT BOLINGER
Palo Alto, California

C. HENRY & BARBARA B. BRADLEY
Dallas, Texas

MARY I. BRESNAHAN
East Lansing, Michigan

BÉLA BROGYÁNYI
Freiburg i.Br., West Germany

ROBBINS BURLING
Ann Arbor, Michigan

JOHN B. CARROLL
Chapel Hill, North Carolina

FREDERIC G. CASSIDY
Waunakee, Wisconsin

JEAN CAUDMONT
Heuchelheim, West Germany

WALLACE CHAFE
Santa Barbara, California

EUGENIO CHANG-RODRIGUEZ
New York, New York

PAUL G. CHAPIN
Washington, D.C.

CHAUNCEY C. CHU
Gainesville, Florida

JOHN A. & MARIE U. CLARK
Ann Arbor, Michigan

D. WELLS COLEMAN
Wildwood, Florida

WALTER A. COOK, S.J.
Washington, D.C.

ELIZABETH & JOHN COSTELLO
Middle Village, New York

GEORGE & FLORENCE COWAN
Huntington Beach, California

J MILTON COWAN
Ithaca, New York

MICHAEL CUMMINGS
Toronto, Ontario, Canada

A. DAVIS
Dallas, Texas

BOYD H DAVIS
Charlotte, North Carolina

LEENA & GYULA DÉCSY
Bloomington, Indiana

FRANCIS P. DINNEEN, S.J.
Washington, D.C.

ROBERT J. & CAROLYN DLOUHY
Kalamazoo, Michigan

WOLFGANG U. DRESSLER
Wien, Austria

BETTY LOU DUBOIS
University Park, New Mexico

CONNIE EBLE
Chapel Hill, North Carolina

STIG ELIASSON
Uppsala, Sweden

RICHARD & BETTY ELKINS
Manila, Philippines

BENJAMIN F. ELSON
Tucson, Arizona

M. B. EMENEAU
Berkeley, California

ENGLISH LANGUAGE INSTITUTE
University of Michigan, Ann Arbor

MARIE FARROW
Manila, Philippines

RALPH W. FASOLD
Washington, D.C.

ROBIN P. FAWCETT
Penarth, United Kingdom

CHARLES A. FERGUSON &
SHIRLEY BRICE HEATH
Palo Alto, California

THE FLOUNDERS

RICHARD W. BAILEY
Ann Arbor, Michigan

DON & PATTY FRANTZ
Alta, Canada

PAUL FRIEDRICH
Chicago, Illinois

PETER & NAN FRIES
Tucson, Arizona

VICTORIA A. FROMKIN
Los Angeles, California

TAKASHI & AIKO FUKUDA
Manila, Philippines

JOENNE GARRETT
Manila, Philippines

WILLIAM J. GEDNEY
Ann Arbor, Michigan

RICHARD & RUTH GIESER
Manila, Philippines

WARD H. GOODENOUGH
Philadelphia, Pennsylvania

ALVAR NYQVIST GOËS
Bromma, Sweden

ANDREW GONZALES, FSC
Manila, Philippines

SIDNEY GREENBAUM
London, England

TOBY D. GRIFFEN
Edwardsville, Illinois

JOSEPH E. & BARBARA F. GRIMES
Ithaca, New York

RICHARD GUNTER
Columbia, South Carolina

AUSTIN HALE
Teaneck, New Jersey

BOB & ALICE HALL
Ithaca, New York

WILLIAM & LEE HALL
Manila, Philippines

ERIC & MARGOT HAMP
Chicago, Illinois

SHIRÔ HATTORI
Yokohama-Shi, Japan

DANIEL P. HENDRIKSEN
Kalamazoo, Michigan

EARL M. HERRICK
Kingsville, Texas

JOHN HEWSON
St. John's, Newfoundland, Canada

KENNETH C. HILL & JANE H. HILL
Tucson, Arizona

CARLETON T. & PATRICIA S. HODGE
Bloomington, Indiana

MELVON J. &
JENNIFER M. HOFFMAN
Buffalo, New York

PETER EDWIN HOOK
Ann Arbor, Michigan

BRUCE & JOYCE HOOLEY
Kangaroo Ground, Victoria, Australia

GEORGE & MARY HUTTAR
Dallas, Texas

FRED WALTER HOUSEHOLDER
Bloomington, Indiana

DELL & VIRGINIA HYMES
Philadelphia, Pennsylvania

FRANCES INGEMANN
Lawrence, Kansas

LARRY B. & LINDA K. JONES
La Porte, Indonesia

BRAJ & YAMUNA KACHRU
Urbana, Illinois

MOVSES & MAIJA KALDJIAN
Ann Arbor, Michigan

ROBERT B. KAPLAN
Los Angeles, California

MARY RITCHIE KEY
Irvine, California

THOMAS P. KLAMMER
Fullerton, California

BYRON J. KOEKKOEK
Buffalo, New York

E. F. KONRAD KOERNER
Ottawa, Ontario, Canada

AMEI KOLL-STOBBE
Freiburg/Br., West Germany

CHARLES W. & CAROL J.
KARDOS KREIDLER
Washington, D.C.

EMMANUEL NWIAH KWOFIE
Lagos, Nigeria

ROBERT L. KYES
Ann Arbor, Michigan

RONALD W. LANGACKER
San Diego, California

D. TERENCE LANGENDOEN
New York, New York

DONALD N. LARSON
St. Paul, Minnesota

ILSE LEHISTE
Columbus, Ohio

RUTH P.M. &
WINFRED P. LEHMANN
Austin, Texas

SAUL & RUTH LEVIN
Binghamton, New York

LINGUISTIC SOCIETY OF
THE PHILIPPINES
Manila, Philippines

DAVID G. LOCKWOOD
East Lansing, Michigan

EUGENE E. LOOS
Dallas, Texas

FLOYD G. LOUNSBURY
New Haven, Connecticut

KEN & JO LUDEMA
Ann Arbor, Michigan

VALERIE & ADAM MAKKAI
Lake Bluff, Illinois

ANDRÉ & JEANNE MARTINET
Sceaux, France

CHRISTIAN MATTHIESSEN
Marina del Rey, California

GEORGE I. MAVRODES
Ann Arbor, Michigan

ERNEST N. MCCARUS
Ann Arbor, Michigan

JAMES D. MCCAWLEY
Chicago, Illinois

HOWARD P. MCKAUGHAN
Honolulu, Hawaii

JOHN & CAROLYN MILLER
Sabah, Malaysia

EDITH A. MORAVCSIK
Milwaukee, Wisconsin

VIRGINIA & RALEIGH MORGAN
Ann Arbor, Michigan

WILLIAM G. MOULTON
Murnau, West Germany

WILLIAM E. NORRIS
Fairfax, Virginia

DAVID OLMSTED
Woodland, California

URSULA OOMEN
Trier, West Germany

DAVID & JUDY OLTROGGE
Dallas, Texas

WESLEY C. PANUNZIO
Westport, Massachusetts

HERBERT H. PAPER
Cincinnati, Ohio

BRUCE L. PEARSON
Columbia, South Carolina

HERBERT & VERA PENZL
Berkeley, California

W. KEITH PERCIVAL
Lawrence, Kansas

L. PÉREZ B.
Saskatoon, Saskatchewan, Canada

VELMA B. PICKETT
Mexico, D.F., Mexico

ROBERT J. DI PIETRO
McLean, Virginia

RICHARD S. & KAY PITTMAN
Waxhaw, North Carolina

DAVID & ELAINE PRESTEL
Okemos, Michigan

PROGRAM IN LINGUISTICS
University of Michigan
Ann Arbor, Michigan

ERNST PULGRAM
Munich, West Germany

STEVE & JANICE QUAKENBUSH
Manila, Philippines

CLEA RAMEH
Washington, D.C.

ROY A. RAPPAPORT
Ann Arbor, Michigan

ALLEN WALKER READ
New York, New York

FRANK & ETHEL ROBBINS
Duncanville, Texas

RICHARD ROE
Manila, Philippines

JOHN S. ROHSENOW
Chicago, Illinois

GLADYS E. SAUNDERS
Charlottesville, Virginia

HANSJAKOB SEILER
Lenzburg, Switzerland

LARRY SELINKER
Ann Arbor, Michigan

JOANNE SHETLER
Manila, Philippines

SEIJI SHIBATA (JUNKO MRS.)
Naruto, Tokushima, Japan

JUNE E. SHOUP
Fallbrook, California

YAU SHUNCHIU
Paris, France

DR. & MRS. BONIFACIO D. SIBAYAN
Manila, Philippines

EVA SIVERTSEN
Dragvoll, Norway

WILLIAM A. SMALLEY
St. Paul, Minnesota

BRIAN D. SMITH
Canterbury, Kent, England

GLENN & MARIE SMITH
Ann Arbor, Michigan

SOUTH PACIFIC SIL SCHOOL
Kangaroo Ground, Victoria, Australia

JAMES C. &
JACQUELINE W. STALKER
East Lansing, Michigan

ERICH H. STEINER
Saarbrücken, West Germany

LENARD STUDERUS
Arlington, Texas

SUMMER INSTITUTE OF LINGUISTICS
Dallas, Texas

OSAMU TAKAHARA
Kobe-Shi, Japan

VERN TERPSTRA &
BONNIE TERPSTRA
Ann Arbor, Michigan

ARNOLD & JUDY THIESSEN
Manila, Philippines

DAVID & DOROTHY THOMAS
Bangkok, Thailand

SANDY & MACK THOMPSON
Santa Barbara, California

EDWARD F. TUTTLE
Los Angeles, California

E. M. UHLENBECK
Voorhout, Holland, The Netherlands

HEINZ VATER
Köln, West Germany

JOHN W. M. VERHAAR, S.J.
Madang, Papua, New Guinea

WILLIAM P-Y. WANG
Berkeley, California

MARGARET WENDELL
Dallas, Texas

BRITT WILLIAMS
LaPorte, Texas

WERNER & INGRID WINTER
Preetz, West Germany

MARY RUTH WISE
Lima, Peru

WOLFGANG WÖLCK
Buffalo, New York

FAY WOUK & PRESTON ASHBOURNE
Mar Vista, California

HAZEL J. WRIGGLESWORTH
Bukidnon, Philippines

BETSY H. WRISLEY
Dallas, Texas

STEPHEN A. WURM
Canberra, Australia

EDWIN H. YOUNG & MRS. YOUNG
Ann Arbor, Michigan

LADISLAV ZGUSTA
Urbana, Illinois

R. DAVID ZORC & MRS. ZORC
Washington, D.C.

ARNOLD M. ZWICKY
Columbus, Ohio